IMAGES
of America

LOCATION FILMING
IN LOS ANGELES

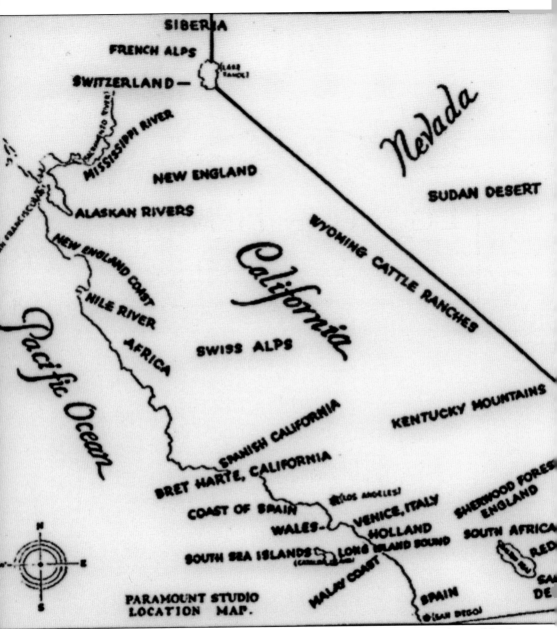

PARAMOUNT STUDIO LOCATION MAP, 1938. Studio location departments used maps like this one to quickly identify areas in California that could double for sites around the world. (Courtesy of Bison Archives.)

ON THE COVER: Harold Lloyd and Bebe Daniels sit suspended above the Hill Street Tunnel in downtown Los Angeles in the Hal Roach production *Look Out Below* (Pathé, 1919). This was Harold Lloyd's first "thrill" picture, where he seamlessly blended comedy with daring stunt work. The terrace and railing were not seen in the movie, giving the illusion that the actors were at a perilous height above the city. (Courtesy of Bison Archives.)

IMAGES
of America

LOCATION FILMING IN LOS ANGELES

Karie Bible, Marc Wanamaker, and Harry Medved

ARCADIA
PUBLISHING

Published by Arcadia Publishing
Charleston, South Carolina

Printed in the United States of America

Library of Congress Control Number: 2010926981

For all general information, please contact Arcadia Publishing:
Telephone 843-853-2070
Fax 843-853-0044
E-mail sales@arcadiapublishing.com
For customer service and orders:
Toll-Free 1-888-313-2665

Visit us on the Internet at www.arcadiapublishing.com

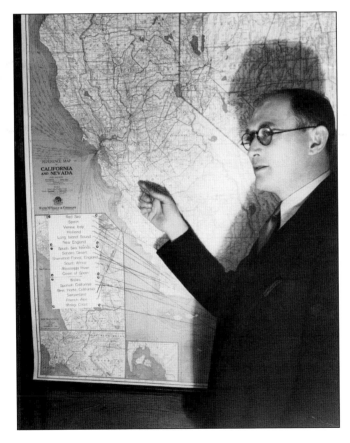

STUDIO LOCATION DEPARTMENT, 1930. Fred Harris, head of the location department at Paramount Studios, shows his map demonstrating that all parts of the world can be found within a radius of 50 miles of Los Angeles. (Courtesy of Bison Archives.)

CONTENTS

ACKNOWLEDGMENTS

Marc Wanamaker began collecting photographs and researching studio history in 1970. In 1971, he founded Bison Archives, which has become the foremost source of images and facts relating to the development of the American film and television industries. The Bison Archive's holdings span more than 100 years of location filmmaking. All photographs and most of the information in *Location Filming in Los Angeles* come from the Bison Archives.

Karie Bible would like to thank the numerous historians whose work has been a great inspiration to her, including Kevin Brownlow, Mark A. Vieira, John Bengtson, David Stenn, Alan K. Rode, Matt Kennedy, Brian Rooney, Mike Malone, Eddie Muller, Emily Leider, Bob Birchard, Andy Erish, Mark Frauenfelder, Thom Andersen, Greg Fischer, Bill Karz, Jim Harris, and Esotouric Tours. Their work has set the highest of standards. She feels fortunate to have learned from each of them. She is eternally grateful to friends who have supported this endeavor, including Mary Mallory, Tom Barnes, Marc Weitz, Mary Stanford, and Sara Henderson. Her contribution on this book is dedicated to her family for their unconditional love and support.

Harry Medved would like to thank his wonderful wife, Michele, and daughters Shoshana and Aviva for their inspiration, encouragement, and patience with his passion for exploring L.A.'s environs. He would also like to thank his *Hollywood Escapes* coauthor Bruce Akiyama and the members of the Location Managers Guild of America (LMGA) for their invaluable support over the years in identifying Southern California's hidden cinematic landmarks.

The three coauthors would also like to thank Arcadia Publishing's diligent editors Jerry Roberts and Ryan Easterling.

This book is dedicated to the entertainment industry's hardworking location professionals who keep the cameras rolling in Los Angeles County.

Introduction

In the early 20th century, Los Angeles was a city of dirt roads, lemon trees, and farmland—a far cry from today's metropolis of 10 million. The fledgling film industry had established studios in New York, Chicago, and Philadelphia. Electric power was still at a premium, so sunlight was needed to expose the slow film stock then in use. Due to rain and snow, filming halted for several months each year.

Knowing that time was wasted and money was lost at unreliable locations, the Los Angeles Chamber of Commerce enticed filmmakers with sunshine. A boastful brochure promised 350 days of sun. Intrigued and desperate, film companies began seasonal treks to Los Angeles. They found the city to be an ideal place to make movies with a host of attributes: inexpensive land, a mild year-round climate, and a diverse geography. Beaches, mountains, deserts, suburbs, and urban landscapes could all be found within close proximity.

In 1907, director Francis Boggs came to California for the Chicago-based Selig Polyscope Company to film a few beach scenes for *Monte Cristo*. Later, in March 1909, Boggs and the Selig company returned to California and set up temporary operations in the drying yard of the Sing Kee Laundry on Olive Street between Seventh and Eighth Streets in downtown L.A.

It was at the Chinese laundry drying yards that Boggs shot the first narrative films made entirely in Los Angeles, including *The Heart of a Race Tout*. Shortly thereafter, they shot one of the first costume dramas in California, *In the Sultan's Power*.

The first permanent film studio in Los Angeles was established by Selig in August 1909, on Glendale Boulevard in the district called Edendale located north of downtown Los Angeles. By 1911, this area was a major center of filmmaking, and it now spans the Echo Park and Silver Lake neighborhoods. There was optimism and excitement in those early days and a sense of community. History was being made.

By 1918 and the end of World War I, the increased demand for movies had made the American film industry a multimillion-dollar business. Film pioneers such as Thomas Ince and David Wark Griffith had brought the motion picture recognition as an art form. Griffith filmed his 1915 *The Birth of a Nation* not in New York or New Jersey, but at his studio on Sunset Boulevard and on location in the Hollywood area. By 1922, there were scores of film companies in Los Angeles, all vying for an international audience and all competing for the city's resources. While larger studios, such as the Fox Film Corporation, had sprawling lots on which to build a variety of exotic settings, many smaller companies were compelled to film entirely on location.

In 1925, after a wasteful stint in Italy, Metro-Goldwyn-Mayer brought its multimillion-dollar *Ben-Hur* back to Los Angeles and recreated Rome on a vacant lot at the intersection of Venice Boulevard and Brice Road (now La Cienega Boulevard). The show-stopping chariot race was one of many epic scenes staged by creative filmmakers in the Los Angeles basin. For a short time, studios such as Paramount shot "talkies" in New York because of Broadway's theatrical community, but Los Angeles remained the hub of filmmaking.

After World War II, the world of filmmaking changed. Lighter, more portable equipment made filming in far-flung locations feasible. Cheap, nonunion labor made it desirable. By the mid-1950s, many of the films set in New York were shot there. Film production had decentralized. A large percentage of Hollywood's output was being filmed in Europe. With the advent of television, the studio system started to crumble. The outsized back lots of MGM and Twentieth Century-Fox were sold to real estate developers in the 1960s and 1970s. Yet the legendary Hollywood with its guilds, soundstages, and film laboratories remained the entertainment capital of the world.

For more than 100 years, the Los Angeles area has been shaped and reshaped to accommodate filmmakers' visions. It has played everything—the old South, Africa, Switzerland, ancient Greece, even outer space. These movie locations are windows into the past, showing us a number of environments that no longer exist. Charlie Chaplin's chase scenes in the 1931 *City Lights* show a Wilshire Boulevard that has changed considerably. The Ambassador Hotel, Bunker Hill, and the downtown Santa Fe Train Station exist only as names, but we can see them on film.

The location images in this book capture a time, a place, and a culture. The book is by no means comprehensive, but it presents a survey of the film landmarks and notable areas from the 1910s through the mid-1970s, when runaway production in Hollywood became an epidemic (a malady we are still fighting to this day).

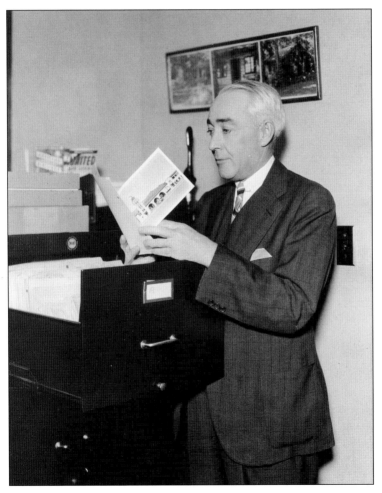

STUDIO LOCATION DEPARTMENT, 1931. R. C. Moore, head of the Fox Film location department, stands beside a filing cabinet that contains thousands of potential location photographs. He holds a photograph of Glendale's Grand Central Air Terminal, a location in the Shirley Temple movie *Bright Eyes*. This building is currently owned by the Walt Disney Company.

One

DOWNTOWN
THE BIRTH OF AN INDUSTRY

The forgotten suburb of Edendale, north of downtown Los Angeles, was where producer William N. Selig and director Francis Boggs opened the first permanent film studio in Los Angeles, the Selig Polyscope Company, in 1909. During the 1910s, many film studios opened in Edendale, erecting structures on Allesandro Street (later renamed Glendale Boulevard).

Edendale welcomed the Keystone Film Company, headed by Mack Sennett in 1912. Between 1913 and 1917, numerous comedy stars worked for Keystone, including Mabel Normand, Charlie Chaplin, Fatty Arbuckle, the Keystone Kops, and Harold Lloyd. Sennett comedies were typically improvised and featured chase scenes filmed in surrounding neighborhoods.

Echo Park Lake, located a mile away from the Edendale studio, was a favorite location for Sennett's unique brand of slapstick comedy. In 1913, when Sennett heard that Echo Park Lake was going to be drained, he mounted a film around it, *A Muddy Romance*.

By the time moviemakers came to downtown Los Angeles, the "Wall Street of the West" had skyscrapers and a bustling street life. With the construction of lavish hotels such as the Biltmore and movie palaces such as the Orpheum, downtown Los Angeles became the movie industry's first stop. Moviemakers made deals on the "Million Dollar Rug" in the lobby of the Alexandria Hotel. Outside, dangerous stunts and thrill scenes were staged by adventurous directors. These pictures offered bird's-eye views of the buildings and streets below.

With its many movie palaces, downtown was the preferred setting for movie premieres until the early 1930s. After World War II, the downtown area started to decline. Scenes filmed there showed poverty, crime, and decay. Bunker Hill, once a neighborhood of regal Victorian homes, fell into disrepair and was demolished by the 1960s.

Many downtown landmarks languished until the late 1990s when civic boosters pushed the area toward a comeback. More than 100 years later, downtown is still a prime filming location representing Big City, U.S.A.

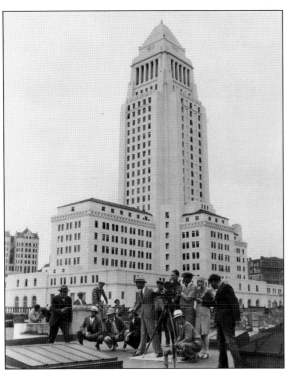

LOS ANGELES CITY HALL, 1928. Lon Chaney films a scene in front of the newly constructed city hall for the silent detective drama *While The City Sleeps* (MGM). The production made great use of downtown rooftops to create the illusion of New York City.

CITY HALL ENVIRONS, 1936. The cast and crew from *Straight from the Shoulder* (Paramount) shoot a scene near First and Spring Streets. In the rear-left background is the new Los Angeles Times Building, dedicated in 1934.

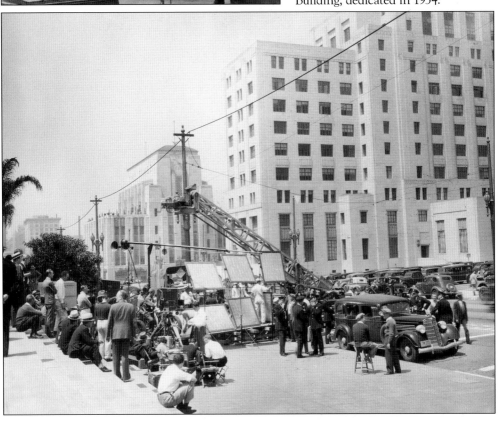

CITY HALL ENVIRONS, 1949.
Loretta Young films *The Accused*
(Paramount) at the Los Angeles
Civic Center with city hall in
the background. City hall has
been featured in numerous crime
dramas, including *Cry Danger*,
L.A. Confidential, and *D.O.A.*,
as well as the opening credits
of television's *Dragnet* and *The
Adventures of Superman*.

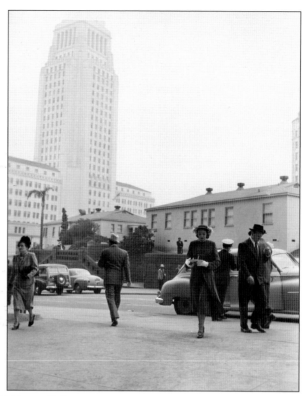

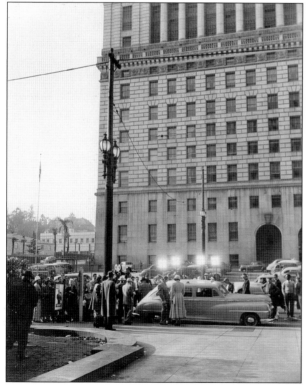

HALL OF JUSTICE, 1949. The
crew for *Illegal Entry* (Universal)
sets up a shot in front of the
1926 Hall of Justice building on
Temple Street, near city hall.
Marta Toren and Howard Duff
stand at the curb waiting to
film their scenes. The Hall of
Justice was also used as a filming
background for the television
shows *Dragnet* and *Get Smart*.

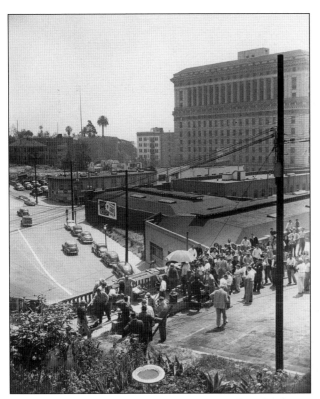

HALL OF JUSTICE ENVIRONS, 1949. The cast and crew of *Criss Cross* (Universal) prepare to film a scene atop the north end of the Hill Street Tunnel, with the Hall of Justice in the background. The film starred Burt Lancaster, Yvonne De Carlo, and Dan Duryea and is widely considered a classic in the film noir genre. The film company shot extensively on Los Angeles streets, many of which no longer exist. The tunnel and hill were later razed to make way for the Civic Center Mall.

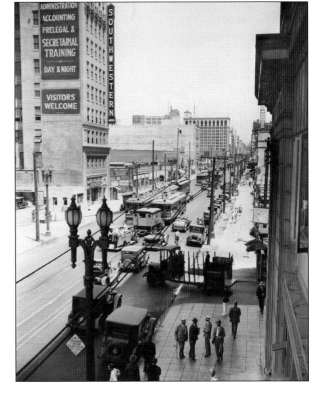

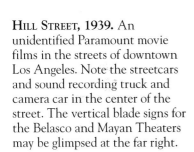

HILL STREET, 1939. An unidentified Paramount movie films in the streets of downtown Los Angeles. Note the streetcars and sound recording truck and camera car in the center of the street. The vertical blade signs for the Belasco and Mayan Theaters may be glimpsed at the far right.

BILTMORE HOTEL, 1927.
Clara Bow and William
Austin stand at the edge of
Pershing Square across from
the Biltmore Hotel while
filming the popular silent
comedy *It* (Paramount).
In more recent times, the
Biltmore has been featured
in *Splash*, *Ghostbusters*,
Wedding Crashers, and
Beverly Hills Cop.

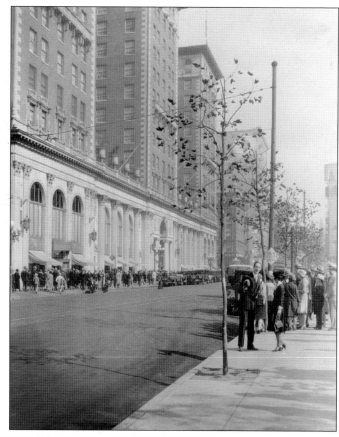

DOWNTOWN, 1929. *The
Mighty*, starring George
Bancroft as a returning war
hero, filmed a scene in front
of the Bartlett Building
at Spring and Seventh
Streets. One of the first
homes of Southwestern
Law School, the Bartlett
has been converted into
fashionable lofts.

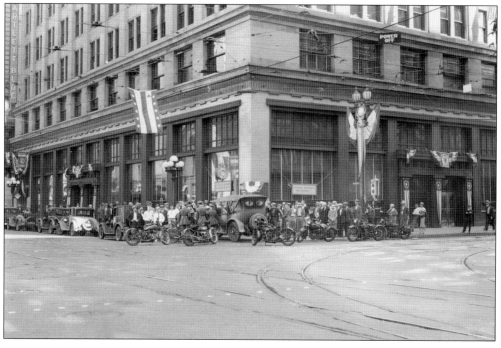

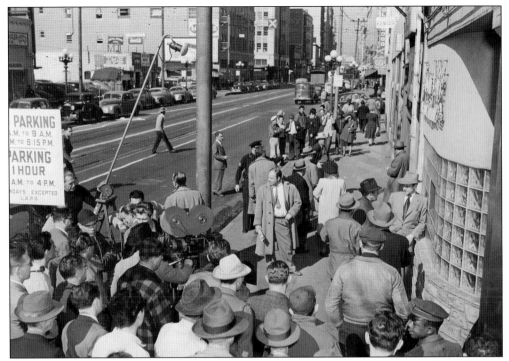

DOWNTOWN, 1949. Tom Drake (leaning on the building at right) receives advice from director Roy Rowland as they prepare to film *Scene of the Crime* (MGM) on South Broadway. The back alleys and busy streets of downtown provided ideal settings for countless film noir productions throughout the postwar era.

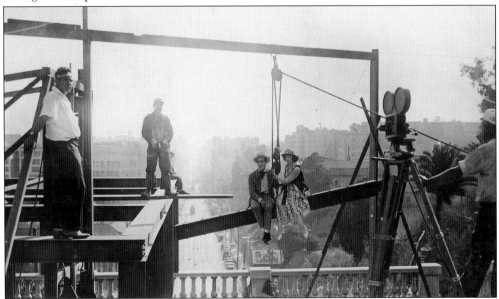

HILL STREET, 1919. Harold Lloyd and Bebe Daniels sit suspended over the south end of the Hill Street Tunnel in the Hal Roach production *Look out Below* (Pathé). Director Hal Roach (at left) placed them on a terrace and when the railing was kept out of the frame, it gave the illusion that they were at a perilous height above the city. Costar Snub Pollard stands in the background.

DOWNTOWN, 1923. Harold Lloyd hangs off the clock in *Safety Last*, which has become one of the most iconic images of the silent era. The scene was filmed in front of a clock set atop the building at 908 South Broadway, at the corner of Ninth Street. A platform was constructed out of frame and camera tricks were utilized to achieve the effects, which are still amazing even today.

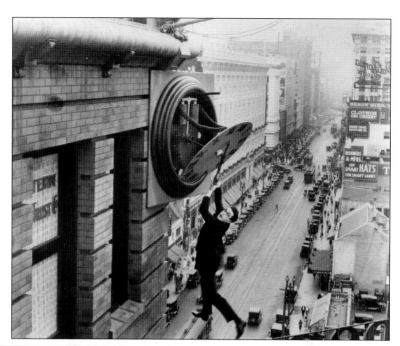

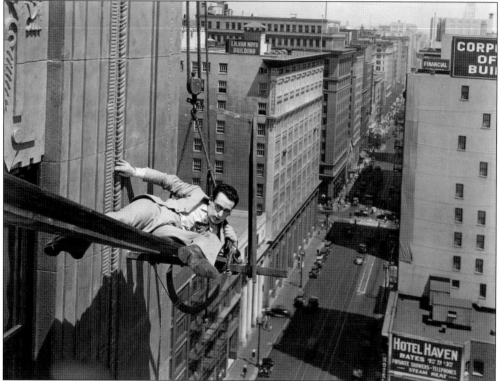

DOWNTOWN, 1930. Harold Lloyd clearly could not stay away from heights as he filmed more daring scenes in *Feet First* (Paramount), which was his last thrill picture. This particular shot, taken from the area near Eighth and Spring Streets, offers a northern view of the Spring Street Financial District.

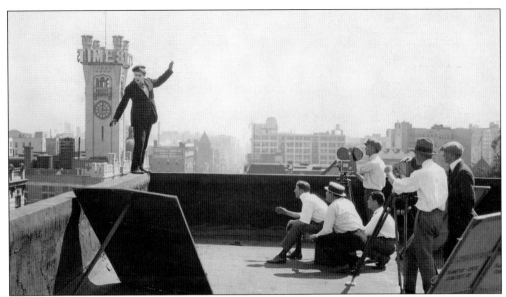

DOWNTOWN, 1922. *Mermaid Comedies* star Lloyd Hamilton is seen here filming on top of a downtown building, performing a dangerous stunt. Film companies in the silent era used rooftops frequently to get the "thrill factor" in their movies. Note the old Los Angeles Times Building in the background. The *Times* tower was located at First Street and Broadway and was dedicated on October 1, 1912.

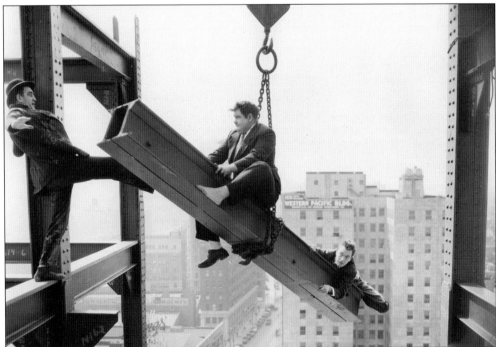

DOWNTOWN, 1929. Laurel and Hardy thrilled audiences with their dangerous stunts in *Liberty* (MGM). The finale of the film was shot atop the downtown Western Costume Building at 939 South Broadway. The scene was filmed on the rooftop of a 150-foot building, upon which a fake three-story-high set was constructed to make it look higher and more perilous.

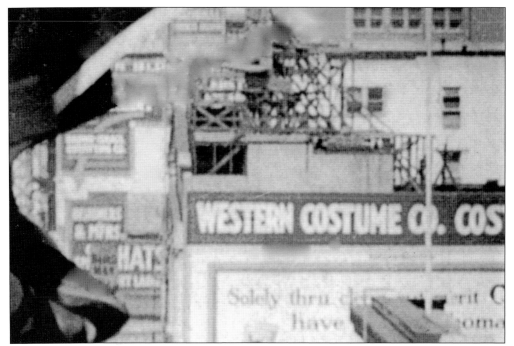

DOWNTOWN, 1924. A special effects camera platform was constructed on the roof of one of the downtown Western Costume buildings, at 908 South Broadway. The platform helped create the illusion of actors hanging or standing on top of buildings overlooking the city streets.

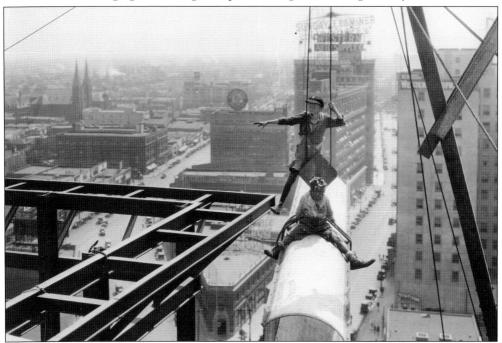

DOWNTOWN, 1927. J. R. Smith and Allen "Farina" Hoskins of "Our Gang" (known to television fans as the Little Rascals) face dangerous heights in the short film Old Wallop (Hal Roach Studios). This was filmed atop the roof of the Western Costume Building at 939 South Broadway.

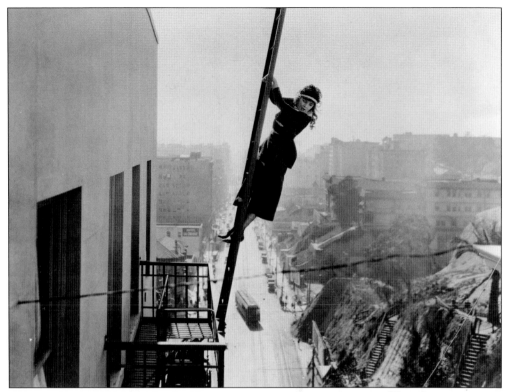

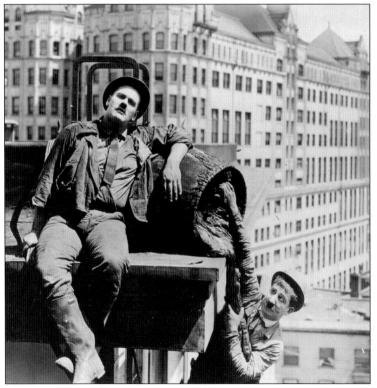

HILL STREET, 1921.
Eileen Sedgwick
hangs from a fire
escape ladder atop
the Hill Street
Tunnel in the
popular serial *Terror
Trail* (Universal).
During the filming
of this scene, Eileen
fell 16 feet into
a tightrope net,
hurting her shoulder.

DOWNTOWN, 1920.
Tar Baby star Hank
Mann hangs from the
new Hotel Broadway
(at Broadway and
Court Street) with
the Los Angeles
Hall of Records in
the background.

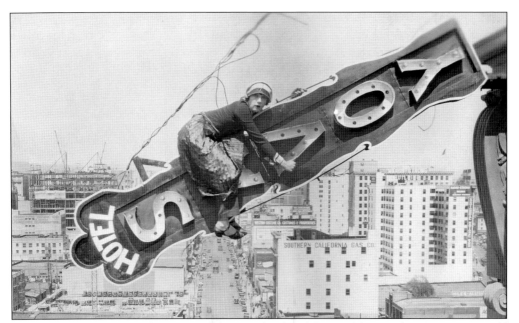

DOWNTOWN, 1924. Dorothy Devore hangs on for dear life to a fake Hotel Savoy sign in *Hold Your Breath* (Christie Film Company). More than 80 years later, *Transformers* would find the evil Decepticons perched atop nearby buildings on Broadway.

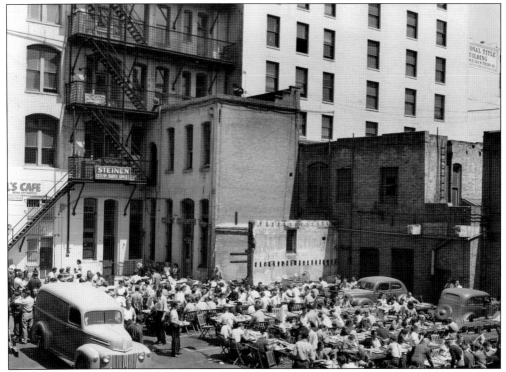

BRADBURY BUILDING, 1944. This candid shot shows the extras eating lunch behind the Bradbury Building, which served as a location for the Irene Dunne melodrama *The White Cliffs of Dover* (MGM). Built in 1893, the Bradbury is located at 304 South Broadway (Third and Broadway).

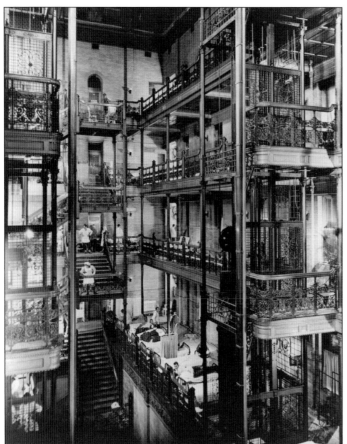

BRADBURY BUILDING INTERIOR, 1944. The Bradbury was transformed into a World War I London military hospital for *The White Cliffs of Dover* (MGM). Its unique design has allowed it to play an exotic hotel (*China Girl*), a futuristic apartment building (*Blade Runner*), a garment factory (M), and an architecture firm (*500 Days of Summer*).

BRADBURY BUILDING, 1953. *I, the Jury* (United Artists) marked the first screen appearance for Mickey Spillane's famed hard-boiled detective Mike Hammer, played here by Biff Elliot. Originally filmed in 3D, the film made great use of the Bradbury's wrought iron and marble stair landings for a climactic fight scene.

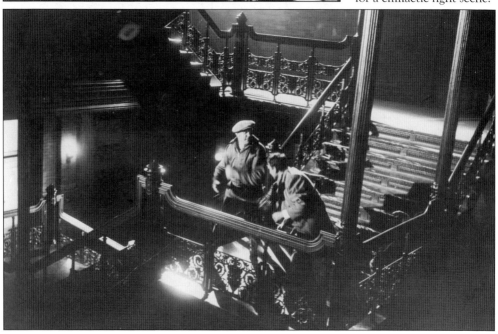

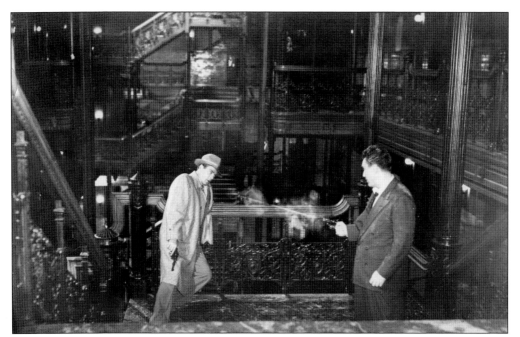

BRADBURY BUILDING, 1950. In the film noir *D.O.A.* (United Artists) Frank Bigelow (Edmond O'Brien) confronts his killer in the Bradbury Building. The building has been used extensively throughout the years in film such as *The Indestructible Man, Murder in the First,* and *Wolf.*

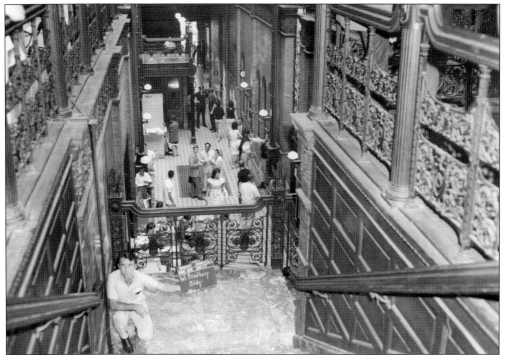

BRADBURY BUILDING, 1969. Director Paul Bogart and crew set up a shot for the screen incarnation of Raymond Chandler's legendary detective in *Marlowe* (MGM). Appropriately, it is now the location for the Los Angeles Police Department's internal affairs division.

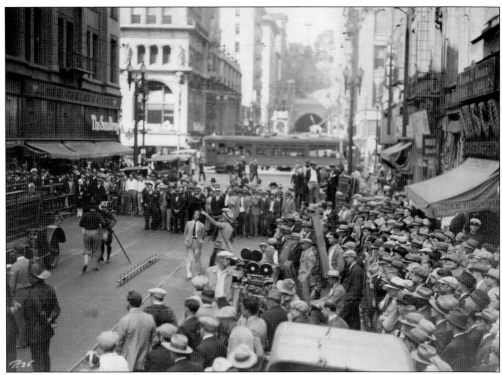

DOWNTOWN, 1929. Numerous extras and onlookers watch as the director readies a scene for the 10-part serial *The Fire Detective* (Pathé). This was filmed on Third Street at Broadway. The Red Car, the Third Street tunnel, and Angels Flight Railway can be seen in the distance.

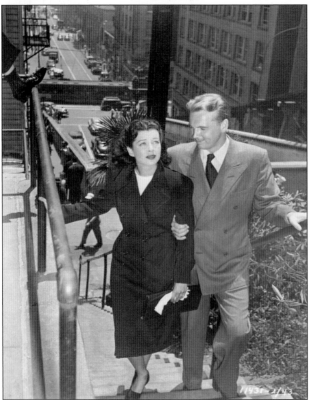

THIRD STREET TUNNEL STAIRWAY, 1948. Gail Russell and John Lund walk up the Third Street tunnel stairway in a scene from the film noir *Night Has a Thousand Eyes* (Paramount), costarring Edward G. Robinson. Angels Flight Railway is at the far right of the photograph.

THIRD STREET TUNNEL ENVIRONS, 1954. James Stewart and Harry Morgan play down-and-out musicians headed for a pawnshop in the opening scene of *The Glenn Miller Story* (Universal). The pawnshop location was on Clay Street, an alley underneath the Angels Flight Railway.

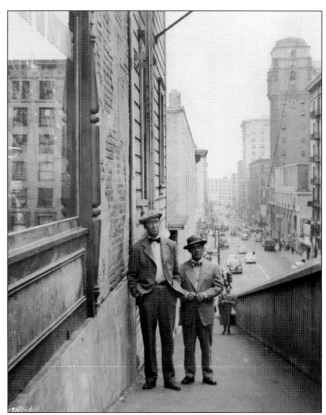

BUNKER HILL, 1949. Parole officer Cornel Wilde ponders the view from his Bunker Hill home in the Samuel Fuller–scripted film noir *Shockproof* (Columbia). Below at the right was the original Los Angeles Police Department headquarters, called the Central Station, located at First and Hill Streets. The station, built in 1896, was demolished in 1955 when Parker Center opened.

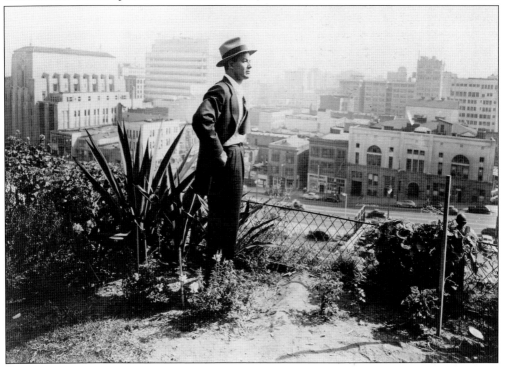

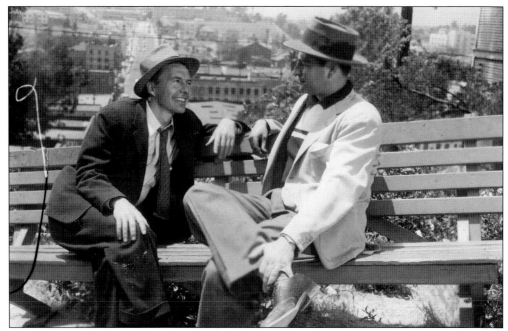

Bunker Hill, 1951. Director Joseph Losey remade Fritz Lang's *M* (Columbia) and set it in the streets of downtown Los Angeles and Bunker Hill. Here actor David Wayne (left, playing the child killer role originated by Peter Lorre) speaks to associate producer Harold Nebenzal while seated on a Bunker Hill bench overlooking the north end of the Third Street Tunnel.

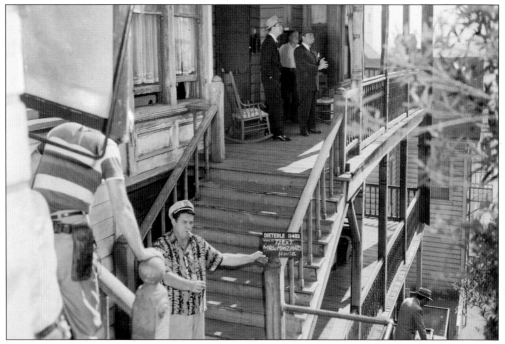

Bunker Hill, 1952. William Dieterle's film noir *The Turning Point* (Paramount), starring William Holden, Edmond O'Brien, and Alexis Smith, filmed at a house above West First Street on Bunker Hill.

OLD CHINATOWN, C. 1920. Italian comedian Monty Banks is ready to drop a bag on the head of a 'heavy' actor in an unknown comedy for Universal. The location was at the rear of Old Chinatown in the alleyways that had not changed since the 19th century.

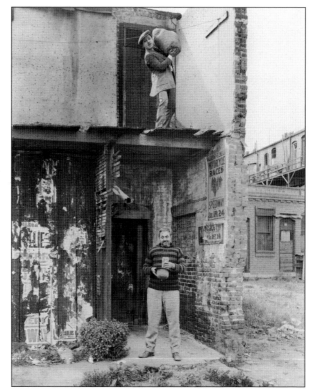

OLD CHINATOWN, 1919. Richard Barthelmess stars as a Chinese immigrant in D. W. Griffith's *Broken Blossoms* (United Artists), filmed on location in Old Chinatown at Marchessault Street, east of Alameda Street.

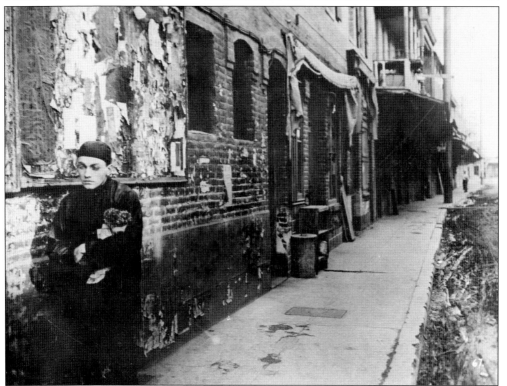

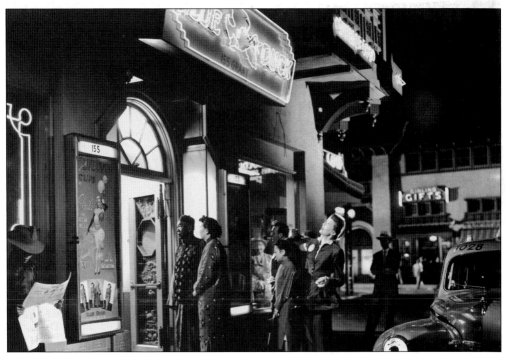

NEW CHINATOWN, 1950. Loretta Young appears in this scene for *Key to the City* (MGM) at a Chinatown nightclub. The New Chinatown was established in the late 1930s when the new Union Station opened on Old Chinatown's original site. The Chinatown area remains a popular location for films like *Chinatown, Lethal Weapon 4,* and *Rush Hour.*

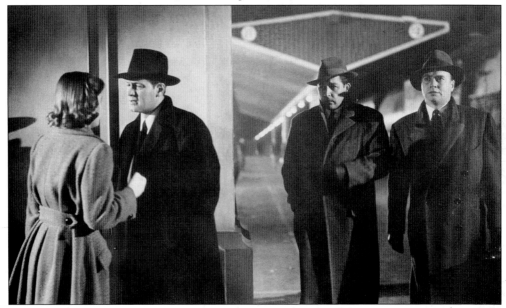

UNION STATION, 1950. William Holden and Nancy Olson starred in *Union Station* (Paramount), shot all around the train platforms, interiors, and exteriors of the location built in 1939 at 800 North Alameda Street across from Olvera Street. It is referred to as the "Last of the Great Railway Stations."

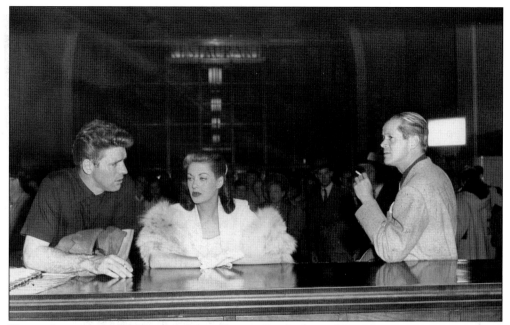

UNION STATION, 1949. Burt Lancaster, Yvonne De Carlo, and Dan Duryea appear in a scene from *Criss Cross* (Universal) at Union Station. Other films to utilize Union Station include *The Way We Were*, *Blade Runner*, and *Bugsy*.

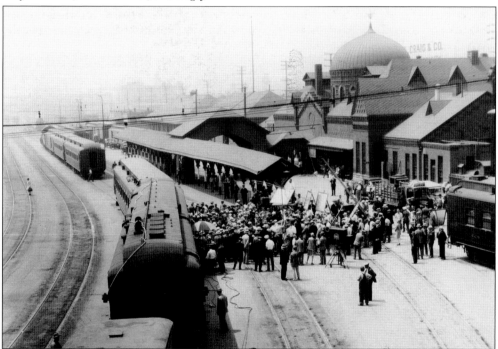

SANTA FE LA GRANDE STATION, 1932. Harold Lloyd used the Santa Fe station at Second Street and Santa Fe Avenue to shoot scenes from *Movie Crazy* (Paramount). Before Union Station was built in the late 1930s, the 1893 La Grande station was one of the main terminals for the city of Los Angeles.

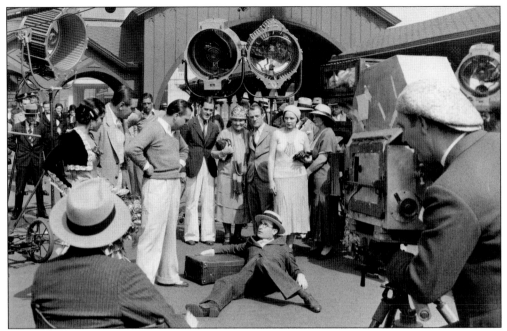

LA GRANDE STATION, 1932. *Movie Crazy* was filmed in actual movie studios and the streets of Hollywood. In this Harold Lloyd talkie, the comedian plays a star-struck Kansas bumpkin arriving at the La Grande depot, where filmmakers offer him a job as an extra.

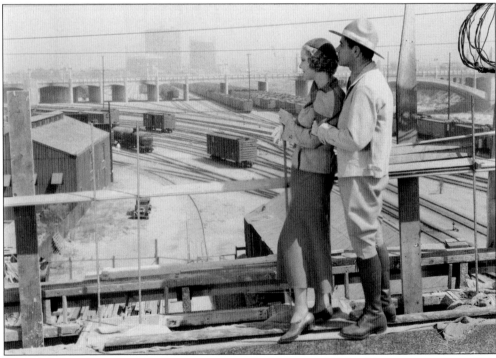

SANTA FE RAIL YARDS, 1932. Ex-con engineer Paul Muni and Helen Vinson survey one of his bridges in *I Am a Fugitive From a Chain Gang* (Warner Bros.). Set in Chicago, this brief scene shows the view looking towards the Fourth Street Bridge and the Santa Fe rail yards.

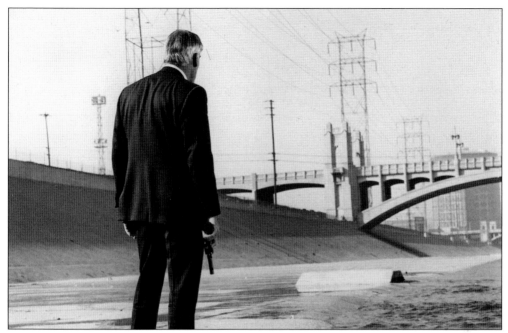

LOS ANGELES RIVER, 1967. Lee Marvin orchestrates a killing below the iconic Fourth Street Bridge (built 1931) in John Boorman's noir classic *Point Blank* (MGM). The Los Angeles River has served as a nest for giant ants in *Them!* and as John Travolta's drag racing site in *Grease*.

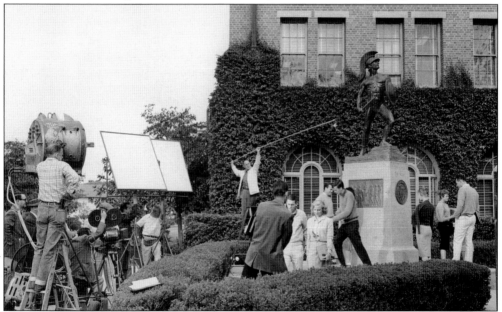

USC CAMPUS, 1962. The cast and crew prepare to film a scene on the University of Southern California campus for the television pilot *You're Only Young Once* (MGM-TV), helmed by USC film school professor and television's *Green Acres* director Richard L. Bare. The bronze school mascot known as *Tommy Trojan* (right) was modeled in 1930 after several USC football players, including future stuntman and production manager Russell Saunders. Other films shot at USC include *The Graduate*, *Road Trip*, and *Legally Blonde*.

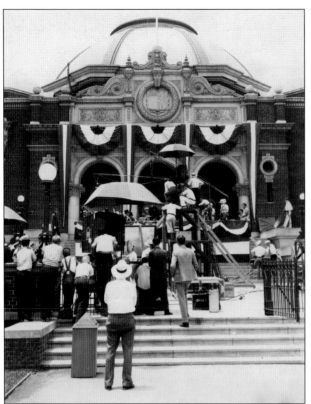

EXPOSITION PARK, 1929. The crew works on location at the Natural History Museum in Exposition Park for *The Mighty* (Paramount), starring George Bancroft and Esther Ralston. It opened in 1913 as a museum of history, science, and art. Decades later, *Spider-Man*'s Peter Parker (Tobey Maguire) gets bitten by a spider in the rotunda's interior.

EXPOSITION PARK, 1938. Edward G. Robinson and Wendy Barrie film a scene for the crime drama *I Am Law* (Columbia) on location at the Natural History Museum steps. The main building (seen to the left) has fitted marble walls and a domed and colonnaded rotunda. The museum is on the National Register of Historic Places.

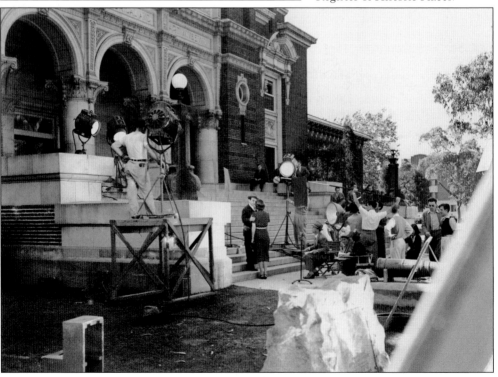

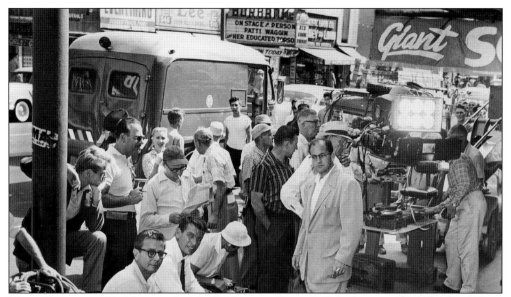

MAIN STREET, 1958. *Voice in the Mirror* director Harry Keller chats with star Richard Egan (seated), who plays an alcoholic lost in this seen-better-days Main Street neighborhood between Fifth and Sixth Streets. The real-life squalor is apparent from the Burbank Theater marquee (at top) announcing the arrival of burlesque dancer "Patti Waggin and Her Educated Torso." Since that time, Main Street has enjoyed a revival, with nearby landmarks Metropolis Books, Canadian Building, Old Bank DVD, Harlem Alley, and the Barclay Hotel appearing in *(500) Days of Summer.*

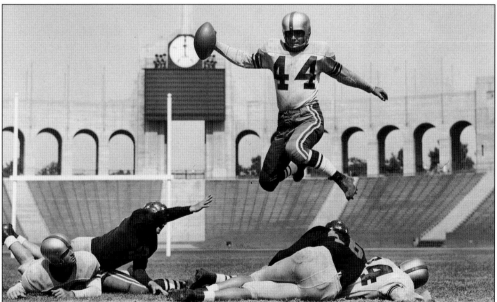

LOS ANGELES MEMORIAL COLISEUM, 1951. John Derek plays a football star in *Saturday's Hero* (Columbia) opposite Donna Reed. The coliseum, located at 3911 South Figueroa Street at Exposition Park, opened in 1923 and hosted the 1932 Olympics. By 1951, it seated more than 100,000 spectators. Since the coliseum was built, the stadium has hosted many productions over the years, making it one of the most filmed locations in Los Angeles.

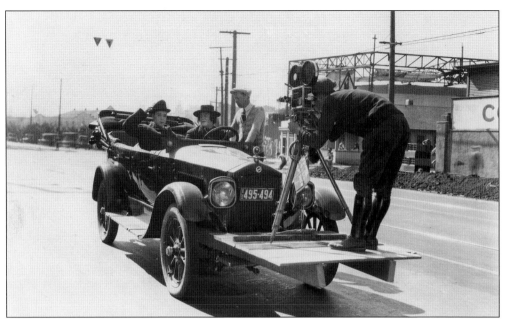

EDENDALE, 1924. Harry Langdon and Vernon Dent film a scene from *All Night Long* in Edendale, across the street from the Mack Sennett Studios located at 1712 Glendale Boulevard. Edendale was where the first film studios were located, dating back to 1909 when the Selig Polyscope Company built the first permanent studio at 1845 Glendale Boulevard.

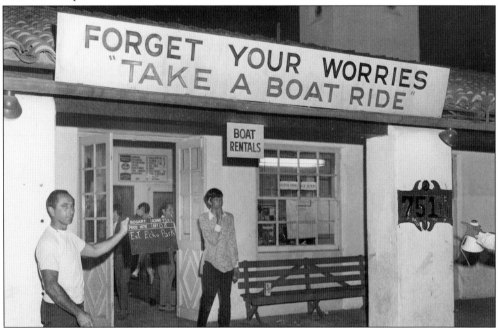

ECHO PARK, 1969. The crew prepares to film a scene at the Echo Park Lake boat wharf for *Marlowe* (MGM), starring James Garner. Years later, another movie gumshoe, J. J. "Jake" Gittes, played by Jack Nicholson, would visit the lake in *Chinatown*. Echo Park Lake has been a popular film location since 1910 when the nearby Selig Polyscope Company used the lake and park as a background.

Two

HOLLYWOOD AND WEST HOLLYWOOD
THE HILLS ARE ALIVE

Hollywood has always been a filmic neighborhood, boasting uniquely recognizable buildings and landmarks, such as Grauman's Chinese Theatre (*Blazing Saddles*), the Capitol Records Building (*Earthquake* and *Hancock*), and, of course, the Hollywood sign (*Escape from L.A.*).

In 1910, D. W. Griffith filmed *In Old California* in the Hollywood Hills and the Cahuenga Pass. This short movie was the first dramatic film shot on location in the Hollywood area. In October 1911, the Nestor Film Company moved from New Jersey to the northwest corner of Sunset Boulevard and Gower Street. This was the first studio located in Hollywood. The first film made by Nestor was *The Law of the Range*.

In December 1913, Jesse Lasky, Samuel Goldfish (later Goldwyn), and Cecil B. DeMille, who were headquartered in New York, rented a barn at the southeast corner of Selma Avenue and Vine Street. Their newly formed Jesse L. Lasky Feature Play Company then produced *The Squaw Man*. Released in 1914, it was the first feature Western made in Hollywood. Two years later, Lasky merged with Adolph Zukor's Famous Players to form Hollywood's first major studio, which later became Paramount Pictures.

Notable locations in the area include Bronson Canyon (*The Searchers*), Runyon Canyon (*Breathless*), Cedar Grove (*The Green Mile*), Vermont Canyon (*Barton Fink*), Griffith Observatory (*Devil in a Blue Dress*), Hollywood Bowl (*Xanadu*), the Greek Theater (*Get Him to the Greek*), the Hollywood Hills (*Double Indemnity*), and the Dresden Room (*Swingers*). These locations are popular to this day, retaining both a unique charm and proximity to the studios.

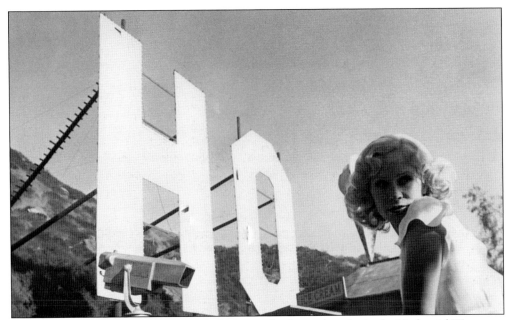

THE HOLLYWOOD SIGN, 1975. Karen Black stars as the doomed starlet in the Nathaniel West story *The Day of the Locust* (Paramount). A replica of the Hollywood sign was built nearby the original sign for easier access since the real Hollywood sign is built on a steep hill. On film, Tinseltown's most iconic landmark serves as a reference point for films about the industry, as in *Ed Wood*, or gets destroyed by natural disasters, as in *The Day After Tomorrow*.

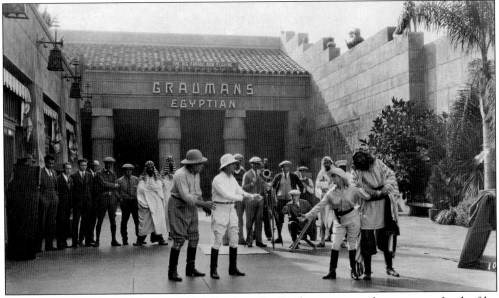

GRAUMAN'S EGYPTIAN THEATRE, 1926. Producer Joe Rock prepares to shoot a scene for the film *Mummy Love* on location in front of the Egyptian Theatre. The film was a Blue Ribbon/Universal release starring Alice Ardell, Neely Edwards, and Gil Pratt. The exotic theater forecourt provided an ideal setting for movie shoots and lavish premieres alike. On October 18, 1922, the Egyptian hosted the star-studded opening of *Robin Hood* (starring Douglas Fairbanks), making it the first Hollywood premiere.

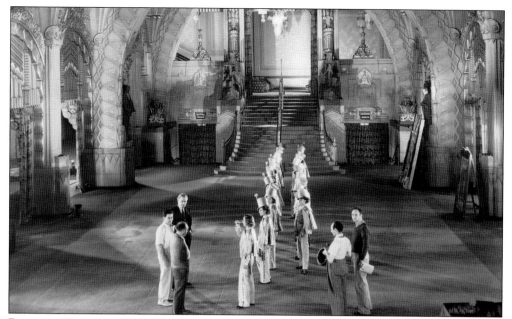

PANTAGES THEATER, 1935. This 1930 art deco movie palace was the location for a scene in *The Good Fairy* (Universal), directed by William Wyler and starring Margaret Sullavan. Here cinema impresario Alan Hale gives marching orders to his army of usherettes in this sophisticated comedy written by Preston Sturges. Now a legitimate theater, the Pantages features one of the most beautiful and lavish lobbies in Los Angeles.

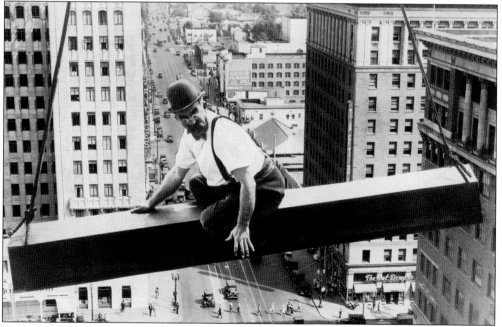

GUARANTEE BUILDING ROOF, 1930. Chester Conklin performs a dangerous stunt for *Cleaning Up* (Paramount) high above Hollywood Boulevard and Vine Street. A special camera platform was constructed atop the newly completed building at Ivar Avenue and Hollywood Boulevard. From this angle, Conklin looks like he is hanging over the street.

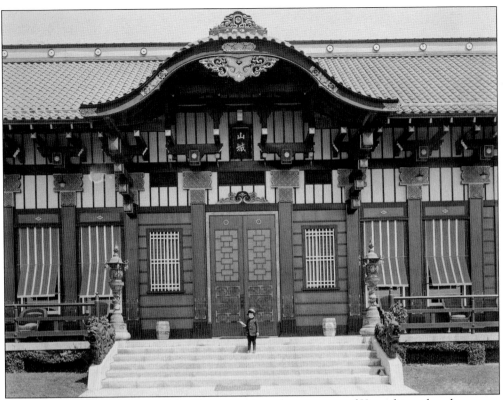

YAMASHIRO, 1921. Child star Baby Peggy stands at the entrance of Yamashiro, then known as the Bernheimer estate. *Yamashiro* means "mountain palace" in Japanese and is an apt description of the location. The Bernheimer brothers were importers of Oriental works of art for many years and opened their authentic Japanese palace on a hill overlooking Franklin and Orange Avenues in 1914. The property appears in *Sayonara*, *Kentucky Fried Movie*, and *Memoirs of a Geisha*.

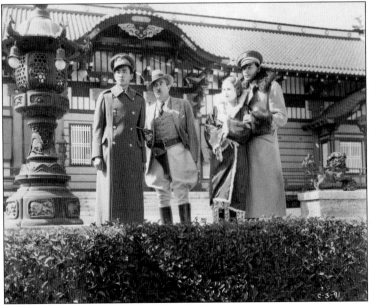

YAMASHIRO, 1933. Hollywood doubled for Shanghai when this private-estate-turned-restaurant was used for this publicity photograph for Frank Capra's *The Bitter Tea of General Yen* (Columbia). From left to right, it starred Richard Loo, Walter Connolly, Barbara Stanwyck, and Nils Asther. Since 1914, the Yamashiro-Bernheimer estate has been one of Hollywood's most unusual landmarks.

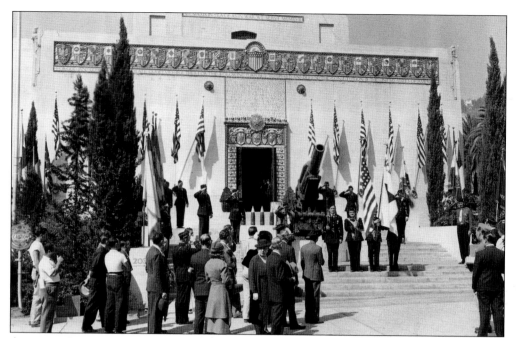

AMERICAN LEGION HALL, 1938. Don Terry, Mary Russell, Thurston Hall, and others film a scene at the American Legion Hall (Hollywood Post 43), located at 2035 Highland Avenue, for the military drama *Squadron of Honor* (Columbia). The American Legion Post building was dedicated on July 4, 1929, and was built for World War I veterans.

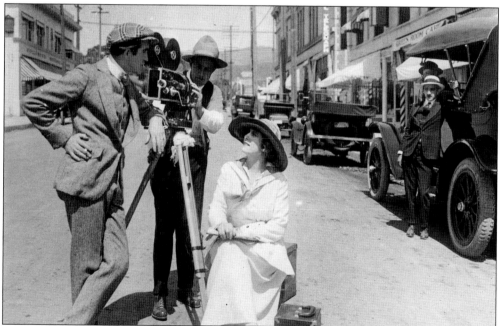

HOLLYWOOD, 1916. Francis Ford and Grace Cunard costar in the serial *The Adventures of Peg o' the Ring* (Universal), filmed at Cahuenga Boulevard looking north to Hollywood Boulevard. Unfortunately, this film is considered to be lost, making this photograph one of the few elements that survives.

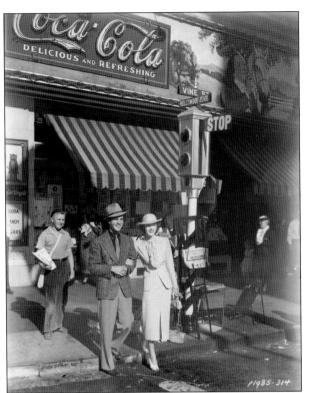

HOLLYWOOD AND VINE, 1936. The most famous intersection in the world takes center stage for a scene in *Hollywood Boulevard* (Paramount). Marsha Hunt and Robert Cummings. cross at the streetlight at the southeast corner of Hollywood Boulevard and Vine Street in front of the Owl Drug Store.

HOLLYWOOD AND CAHUENGA BOULEVARDS, 1923. Harold Lloyd films a scene on location for *Why Worry?* (Pathé) at the northwest corner of Hollywood and Cahuenga Boulevards. Charlie Chaplin filmed scenes near the southwest corner of this same intersection for *Tillie's Punctured Romance* in 1914.

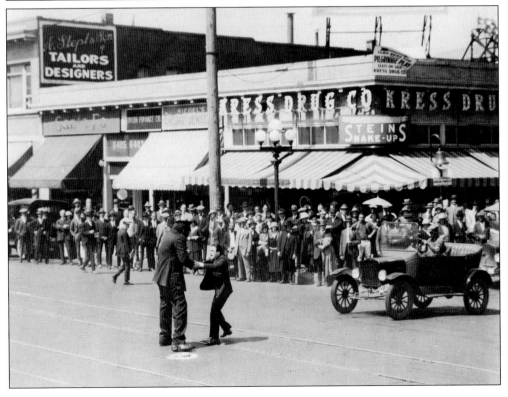

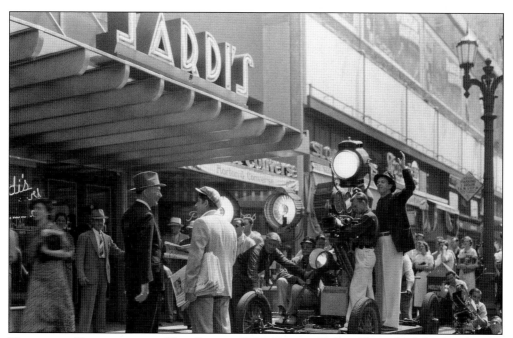

HOLLYWOOD BOULEVARD AND VINE STREET, 1936. Director Robert Florey (with his hand in the air) sets up a shot for the film *Hollywood Boulevard* (Paramount) in front of the L.A. branch of famed restaurant Sardi's, designed in 1932 by Rudolph Schindler. Behind the camera platform is part of the now-demolished 1933 Laemmle Building (designed by Richard Neutra), which was on the northwest corner of Hollywood Boulevard and Vine Street.

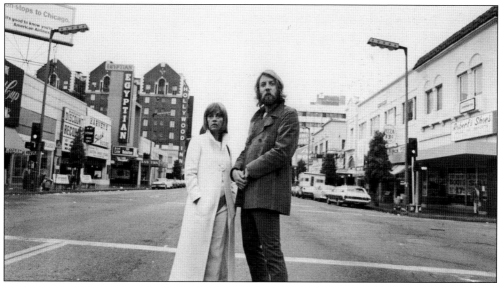

HOLLYWOOD AND LAS PALMAS, 1970. Jeanne Moreau and Donald Sutherland stand at the intersection of Hollywood Boulevard and Las Palmas Avenue during the making of the film *Alex in Wonderland* (MGM). The film's Fellini-esque story concerns a director struggling with his next project, while exploring the social issues of the time. Visible behind them is the marquee for the Egyptian Theatre, now home of the American Cinematheque, which screens films from all over the world.

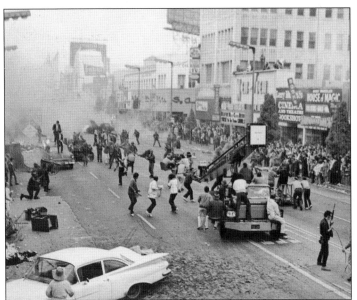

HOLLYWOOD BOULEVARD, 1970. Paul Mazursky's *Alex in Wonderland* (MGM) featured an incredible fantasy sequence showing the filming of a battle scene on Hollywood Boulevard. Note in the background the Hollywood Center Building (first SAG headquarters), House of Magic, and Larry Edmunds Cinema and Theatre Bookshop, which specializes in film books and has been a favorite of filmmakers Francois Truffaut and Quentin Tarantino.

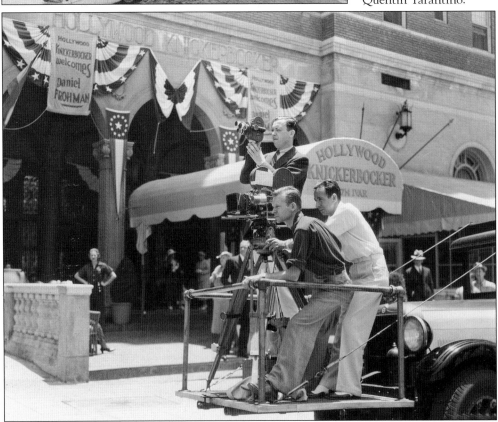

IVAR STREET, 1936. Paramount director Robert Florey (standing, holding small camera) directs the photographing of Hollywood streets, which will be used as a background for *Hollywood Boulevard* (Paramount). They are filming on Ivar Street in front of the Hollywood Knickerbocker Hotel, a local landmark built in 1925.

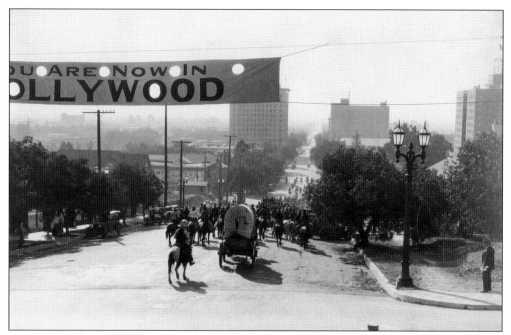

NORTH VINE STREET, 1926. This scene from *Miss Brewster's Millions* (Paramount), starring Bebe Daniels, was shot on Vine Street at Franklin Avenue looking south to Hollywood Boulevard, near the site of today's Capitol Records Building. This photograph shows the pepper trees that used to line Vine Street all the way to the Taft and Dyas Buildings at Hollywood Boulevard and Vine Street, near today's W Hotel.

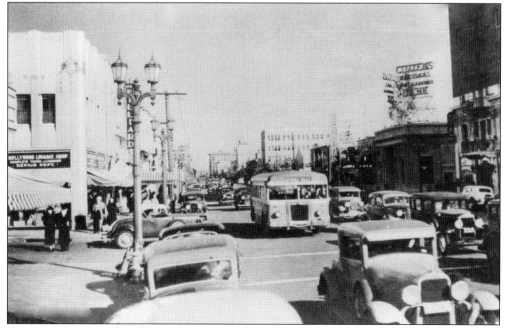

HOLLYWOOD, 1937. The film *A Star is Born* (United Artists) shot at locations all throughout Hollywood and starred Janet Gaynor and Fredric March. This publicity still shows Hollywood Boulevard looking east from Highland Avenue.

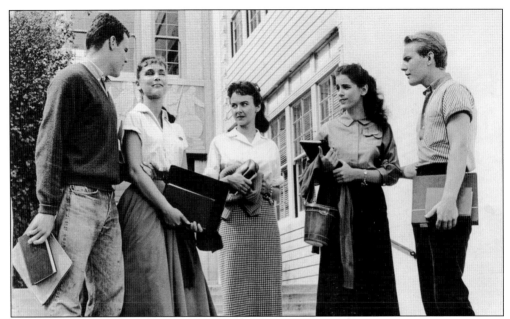

Hollywood High School, 1957. One of the most famous high schools in the world, Hollywood High (1521 North Highland Avenue) was the location for the social issue film *Eighteen and Anxious* (Republic). It has also been used as a location for *Foxes, Better Off Dead,* and *Nancy Drew.* Hollywood High is the alma mater of such show business luminaries as Carol Burnett, Judy Garland, Ricky Nelson, Lana Turner, Sally Kellerman, John Ritter, Rita Wilson, Laurence Fishburne, and director Frank Darabont.

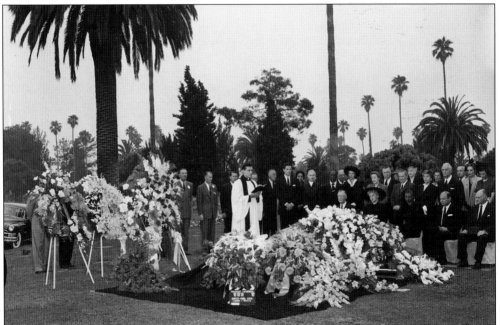

Hollywood Memorial Park, 1956. A funeral scene from the film *The Scarlet Hour* was directed by Michael Curtiz and shot at Hollywood Memorial Park Cemetery, now renamed Hollywood Forever. Other films shot on the grounds include *The Player, L.A. Story, Valentine's Day,* and *The Prestige.*

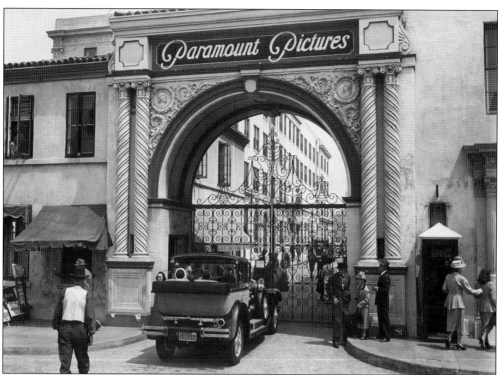

PARAMOUNT'S BRONSON GATE, 1950. Erich von Stroheim drives Gloria Swanson and William Holden through the Paramount Bronson gate for a scene in *Sunset Boulevard* (Paramount). This 1926 gate became one of Paramount's iconic symbols by 1930. Located near the intersection of Melrose and Bronson Avenues, it is no longer the studio's main entrance and is now inaccessible to the public. Character actor Charles Buchinsky was said to have been inspired by the Bronson Gate when he picked his new stage name (for which he was better known by), Charles Bronson.

MELROSE AVENUE, 1962. Bette Davis, director Robert Aldrich, and crew prepare to film scenes for *What Ever Happened to Baby Jane?* (Warner Bros.) in front of the Hollywood Western Costume Company Building at 5339 Melrose Avenue, adjacent to Paramount.

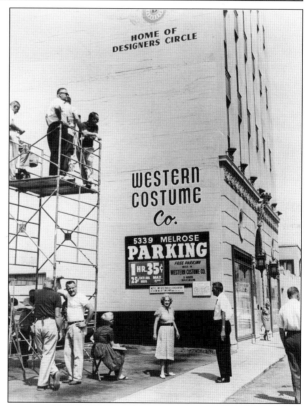

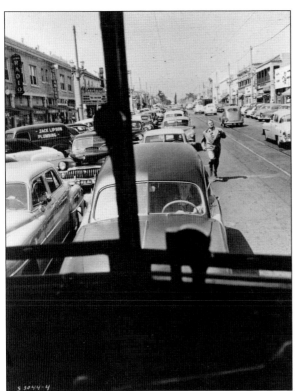

LARCHMONT VILLAGE, 1952.
Comic filmmaker Pete Smith
took to the streets to film a short
called *Pedestrian Safety* (MGM).
His "Pete Smith Specialties"
were a popular series of shorts
that covered a variety of topics.
Larchmont Village is central to
Hollywood and has appeared in
the Three Stooges comedies *Punch
Drunks* (1934), *Pop Goes the Easel*
(1935), and *Hoi Polloi* (1935).

**MELROSE AVENUE AND HELIOTROPE
DRIVE, 1930.** Comedy star Mack
Swain prepares to shoot a scene
for *Cleaning Up* (Paramount) on
location near the former campus
of the University of California,
Los Angeles (UCLA), shortly after
the school's move to Westwood in
1929. Los Angeles City College now
stands on the original UCLA site.

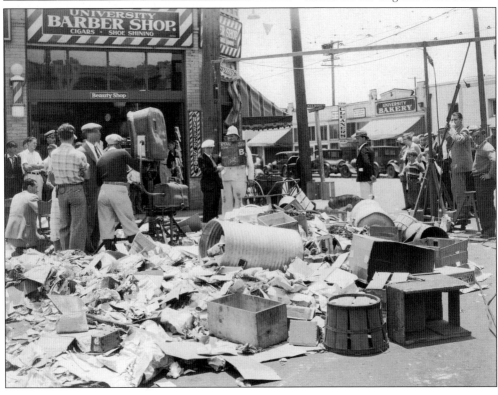

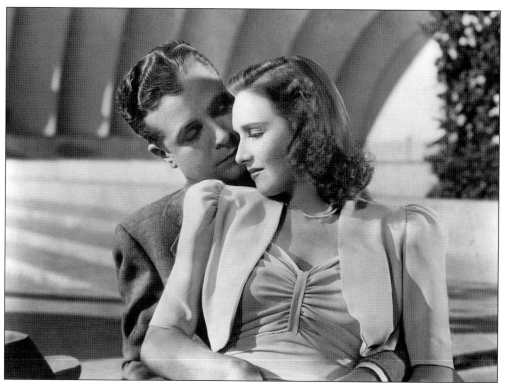

HOLLYWOOD BOWL, 1938. Dick Powell stars alongside Rosemary Lane in *Hollywood Hotel* (Warner Bros.), directed by Busby Berkeley. Other film credits for the famed Hollywood Bowl include *A Star is Born* (1937), *Anchors Aweigh*, *Beaches*, and *Some Kind of Wonderful*.

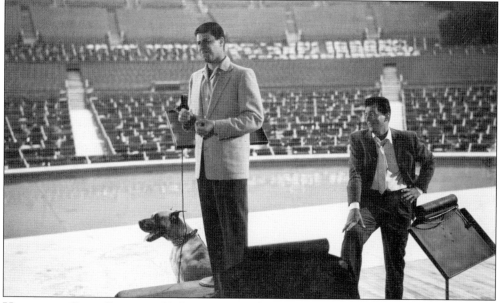

HOLLYWOOD BOWL STAGE, 1956. Jerry Lewis and Dean Martin film a scene at the Hollywood Bowl for the comedy *Hollywood or Bust* (Paramount). Note the pool in front of the bowl stage. It was later taken out for expanded seating.

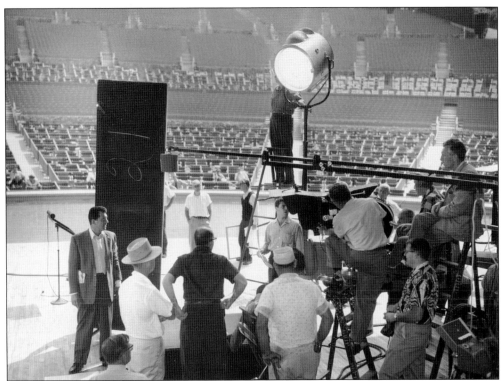

HOLLYWOOD BOWL, 1956. The crew sets up a scene with Jerry Lewis and Dean Martin in *Hollywood or Bust* (Paramount). This film marked their final appearance as a comedy team.

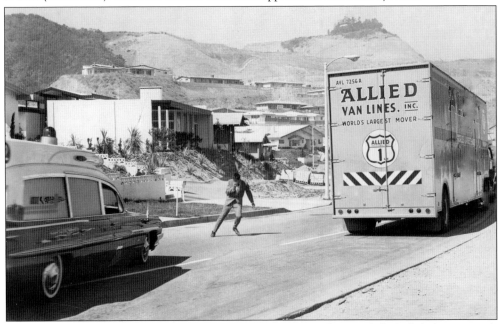

HOLLYWOOD HILLS, 1964. Jerry Lewis dodges an ambulance in *The Disorderly Orderly* (Paramount), which filmed the climatic chase in the Laurel Canyon vicinity near Laurel Pass Avenue. This scene was shot in a new development in between Lookout Mountain Avenue and Mulholland Drive.

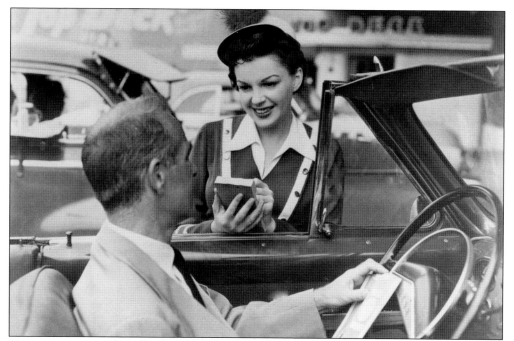

HOLLYWOOD, 1954. Judy Garland stars as a drive-in waitress who becomes a movie star in *A Star is Born*. This scene was shot at Top Deck Drive-In on Sunset and Cahuenga Boulevards, which had previously been the site of several other drive-in restaurants. The site today is located across the street from Amoeba Records and the ArcLight Cinemas and Cinerama Dome complex.

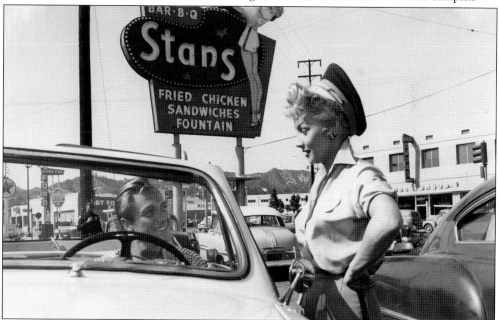

EAST HOLLYWOOD, 1955. Richard Denning, seated behind the wheel of the car, and Mari Blanchard, playing a carhop, are pictured on location for *The Crooked Web* (Columbia) at Stan's Drive In Restaurant on Sunset Boulevard and Virgil Avenue. Stan's was located across the street from the Vista Theater at the intersection of Hillhurst Avenue, Sunset Boulevard, and Virgil Avenue.

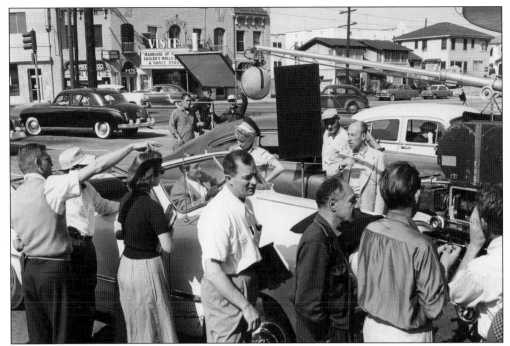

VISTA THEATER, 1955. Mari Blanchard films a scene from *The Crooked Web* (Columbia) near the Vista Theater, seen in the background. Built in 1923, the theater sits on land that was once the site of the famous Babylon sets of D. W. Griffith's 1916 epic *Intolerance*.

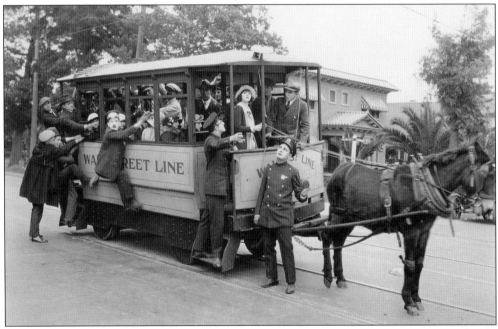

FRANKLIN AVENUE, 1922. Jobyna Ralston and James Parrott costar in the Hal Roach comedy *The Next Car* (Pathé). Note the street signs for Franklin and Bronson Avenues, partially glimpsed behind the horse in this photograph. At this time there were no horse-drawn trolley cars left in the city, so the famous Hal Roach Studio prop and miniature department built one for use in the film.

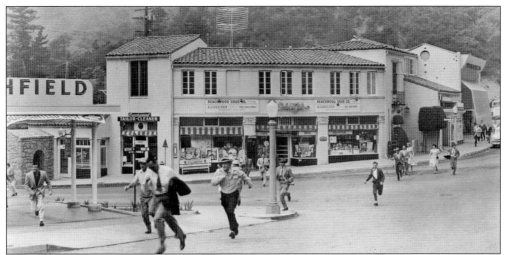

Beachwood Drive, 1956. Alien "Pod People" are on the march in *Invasion of the Body Snatchers* (Allied Artists). This classic thriller filmed its Santa Mira scenes near the Village Coffee Shop and the Beachwood Market (pictured here) and in many other locales, including Bronson Canyon and the Kersting Court town square in the San Gabriel foothill village of Sierra Madre.

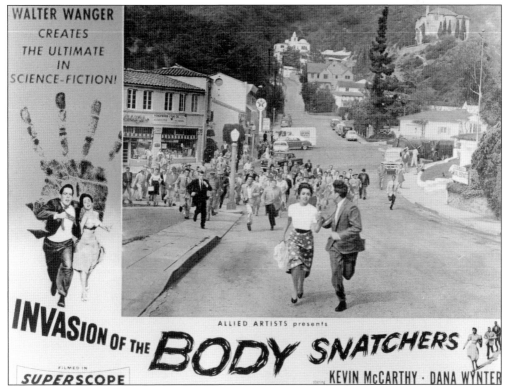

Beachwood Canyon, 1956. Don Siegel's *Invasion of the Body Snatchers* (Allied Artists) was shot to make Hollywood's Beachwood Canyon feel like small-town America. The intersection of Westshire, Beachwood, and Belden Drives appeared in another 1956 body-snatching movie, Roger Corman's *It Conquered the World*.

49

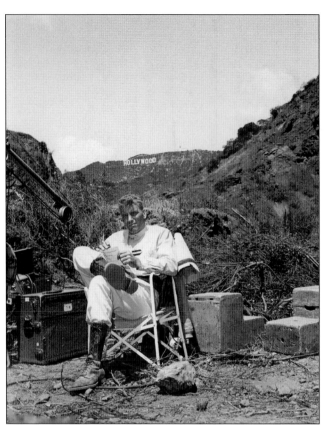

BRONSON CANYON, 1951. Burt Lancaster, costumed as a French foreign legionnaire, sits below the Hollywood sign in between takes on the film *Ten Tall Men* (Columbia). Bronson Canyon, with its cliffs, caves, and rugged terrain, has been in use as a movie location since 1912.

GRIFFITH PARK, 1973. Griffith Park stands in for Africa as the director positions the natives under the Hollywood sign in the remake of *Trader Horn* (MGM). The photograph caption was labeled "Africa West," a reference to the ability of Hollywood area locations to represent all corners of the world.

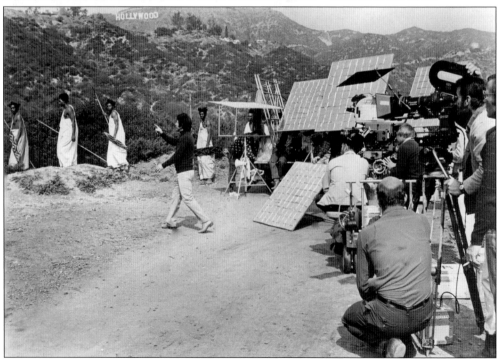

BRONSON CANYON, 1953.
Marlon Brando, uniformed as Roman general Mark Antony, waits for his cue to lead the battle in Joseph L. Mankiewicz's *Julius Caesar* (MGM). Other classic films that shot scenes at this Hollywood Hills location include John Ford's *The Searchers* (when John Wayne tells Natalie Wood, "Let's go home, Debbie") and Sam Peckinpah's *Ride the High Country* (the mining camp sequence).

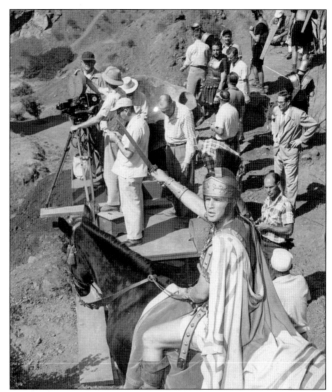

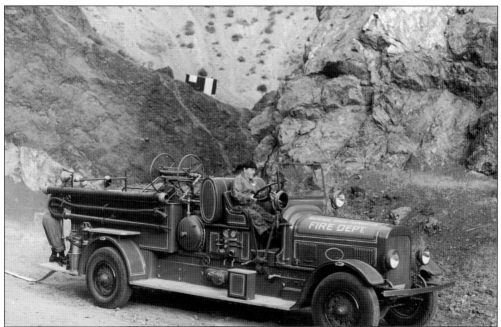

BRONSON CANYON, 1959. The Three Stooges (Moe Howard, Larry Fine, and Joe De Rita) prepare to fight a fire in *Have Rocket, Will Travel* (Columbia). Located at the end of Canyon Drive in a former Griffith Park rock quarry, Bronson Cave appears in the comedies *Sleeper, Head, Strange Wilderness,* and *The Lost Skeleton of Cadavra.*

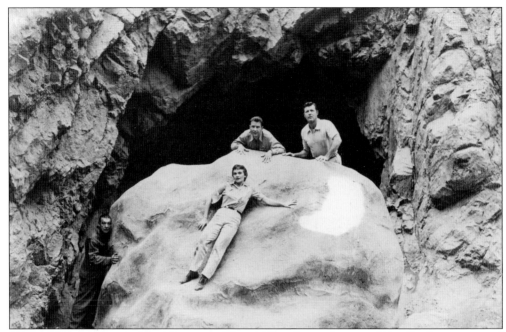

BRONSON CANYON, 1957. Lon Chaney Jr., Gloria Talbot, James Craig, and Tom Drake are pictured at the mouth of the Bronson Cave in Bert I. Gordon's *The Cyclops* (RKO). Bronson was a favorite lair for numerous 1950s B-movie creatures like *The Spider, The Brain from Planet Arous,* and the immortal *Robot Monster,* a gorilla wearing a deep-sea diving helmet.

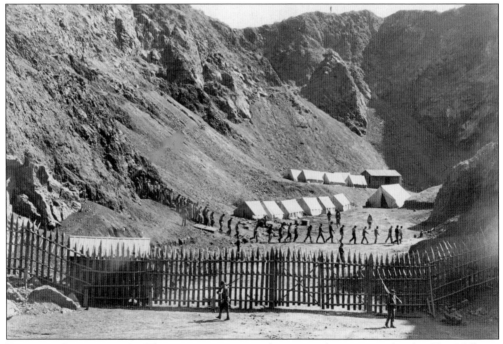

BRONSON CANYON, 1952. The canyon was turned into a military camp for the film *Hellgate,* starring Sterling Hayden and Ward Bond. The canyon made an excellent outdoor setting with a natural background that doubled for a Civil War–era New Mexican prison.

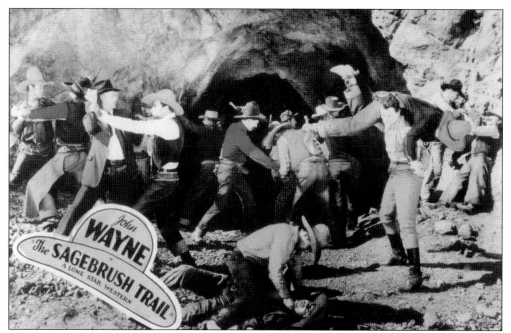

BRONSON CANYON, 1933. A young John Wayne prepares to toss a cowboy off his shoulders in a Bronson Canyon fight from *The Sagebrush Trail* (Monogram Pictures). The Bronson Cave, a setting for hideouts, prehistoric landscapes, and alien planets, is best known as The Bat Cave from television's *Batman*.

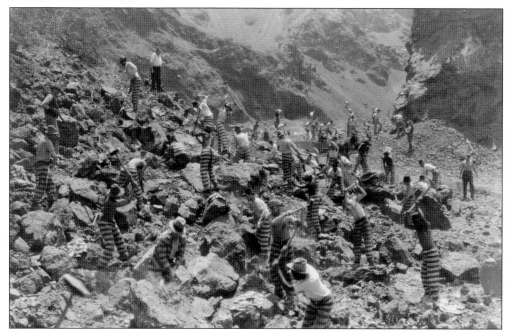

BRONSON CANYON, 1932. Prison camp workers hammer rocks in *I Am a Fugitive From a Chain Gang* (Warner Bros.) at Bronson Canyon, once a quarry for building the rail beds for the Pacific Electric in the Los Angeles area. From the Warner Bros. Sunset studio, it took all of 10 minutes of travel time to commute to this location.

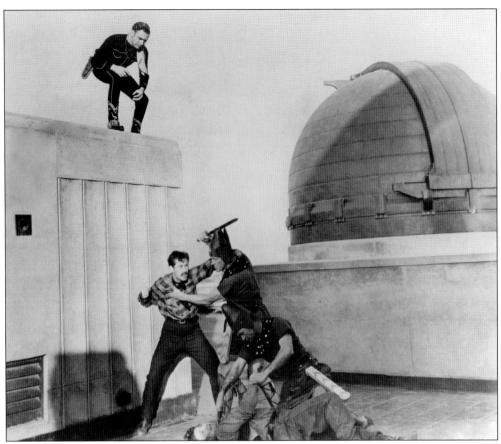

GRIFFITH OBSERVATORY, 1935. Gene Autry starred as a futuristic radio star/cowboy in the bizarre serial *The Phantom Empire* (Mascot Pictures). Due to its forward-looking art deco architecture, Griffith Observatory has become a popular filming location for sci-fi movies like *The Terminator*, *The Rocketeer*, and *Transformers*.

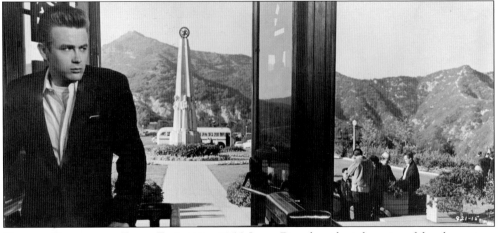

GRIFFITH OBSERVATORY FRONT ENTRANCE, 1955. James Dean broods at the entry of the observatory in *Rebel Without a Cause* (Warner Bros.). A bust of James Dean has since been placed there to memorialize the film and its legendary star.

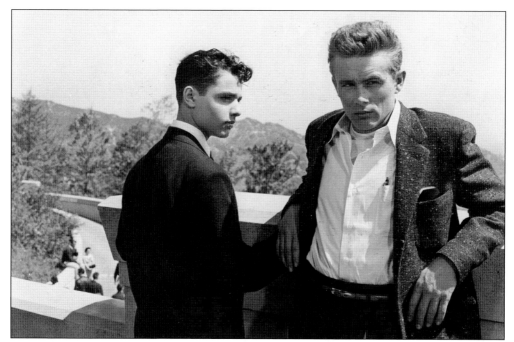

GRIFFITH OBSERVATORY, 1955. James Dean and Sal Mineo costar in *Rebel Without a Cause* (Warner Bros.). A large portion of the film was shot on location in and around the observatory, including the planetarium scene, the knife fight, and the climatic shoot-out.

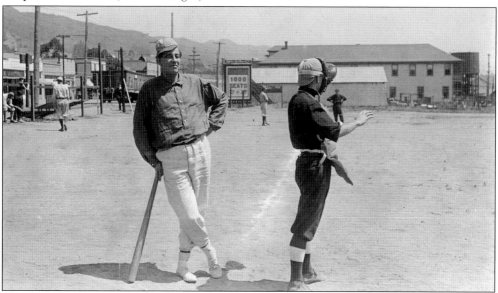

WEST HOLLYWOOD PARK, 1916. DeWolf Hopper stands at the plate for *Casey at the Bat* (Fine Arts), filmed in the town of Sherman, California (now known as West Hollywood). This scene was shot at Sherman's baseball park, located at the intersection of Santa Monica and Robertson Boulevards. Note in the background the Sherman rail yards and Sherman Junction, where the Pacific Electric and freight trains were a common feature of the town. Today this recreational area is known as West Hollywood Park and includes a library, baseball diamonds, a swimming pool, and a community center fronting San Vicente Boulevard.

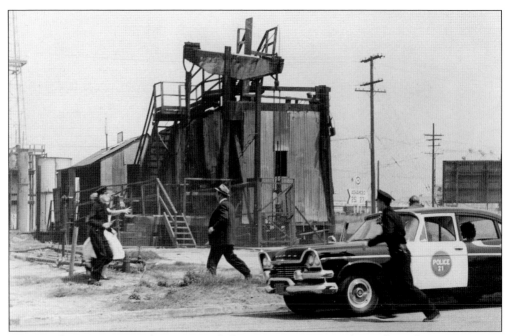

BEVERLY CENTER, 1959. Police arrive to help a woman in a scene from *The Hideous Sun Demon* (Pacific International) at the Beverly Oil Fields, once located between the intersections of Beverly and San Vicente Boulevards and Third Street and LaCienega Boulevard. The oil pump in this shot continues to yield oil and is hidden behind the Beverly Center on San Vicente Boulevard.

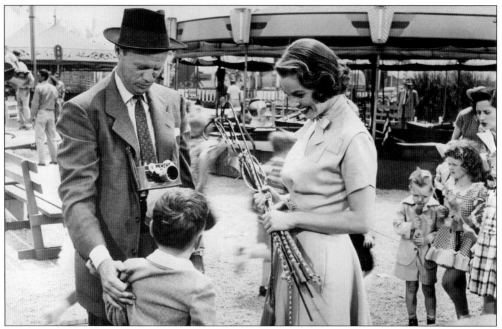

BEVERLY PARK, 1952. Richard Widmark films a scene in front of Beverly Park for the film *My Pal Gus* (Twentieth Century-Fox). Beverly Park was originally a children's amusement park established in 1945 on the Beverly Oil Company property on the southwest corner of La Cienega and Beverly Boulevards, site of today's Beverly Center.

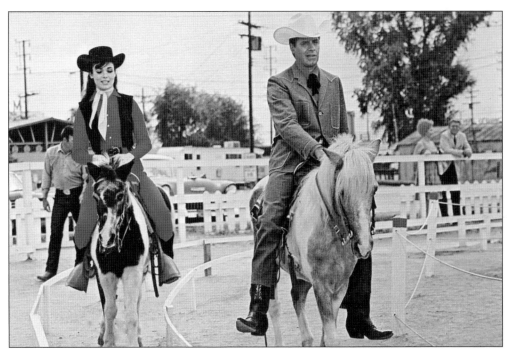

PONYLAND, 1966. Jerry Lewis saddles up at Ponyland for the film *Three on a Couch* (Columbia). Adjacent to Beverly Park, the children's attraction was located at the southeast corner of Beverly and San Vicente Boulevards. Opened around the same time as Beverly Park, Ponyland became a popular attraction for Hollywood stars and celebrities.

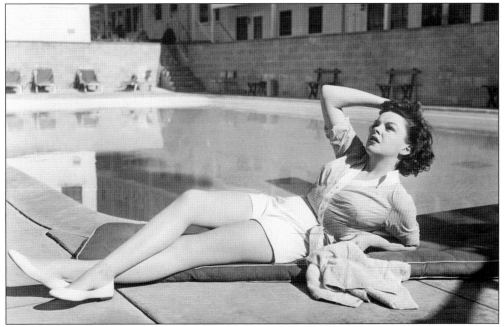

WEST HOLLYWOOD, 1954. During the making of *A Star is Born* (Warner Bros.), Judy Garland suns herself poolside on location at the Oleander Arms apartments at the southeast corner of Fountain Avenue and Crescent Heights Drive.

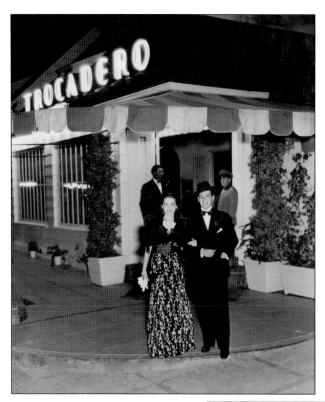

SUNSET STRIP, 1936. John Halliday and Creighton Hale film a scene in front of the famed Café Trocadero at 8610 Sunset Boulevard, near Sunset Plaza Drive, for the movie *Hollywood Boulevard* (Paramount). The Trocadero was the most popular restaurant-nightclub in Los Angeles from 1936 until its closing in 1946. Other famous clubs on the strip used as film locations included Mocambo, Clover Club, and Ciro's (today the site of The Comedy Store).

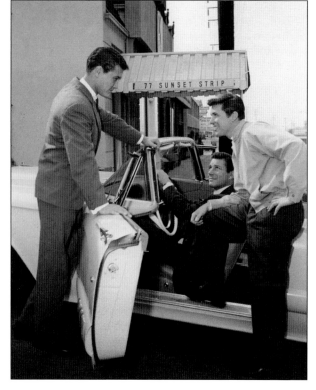

SUNSET STRIP, 1958. Roger Smith, Ed "Kookie" Byrnes, and Efrem Zimbalist Jr. film a scene in front of Dino's Lodge (Dean Martin was a short-lived partner in the business) at 8524 Sunset Boulevard in the television series *77 Sunset Strip* (Warner Bros.). The driveway was where much of the action took place outside of the restaurant-club.

Three

MALIBU TO LONG BEACH
LOS ANGELES COUNTY COAST

The Pacific Ocean has always been a draw for filmmakers, from the frolics of Mack Sennett's Bathing Beauties at Venice and Santa Monica to Michael Bay's high-octane chase scenes shot in the harbortown streets of San Pedro and Long Beach.

Venice was planned by tobacco baron Abbot Kinney as an American version of the Italian city, complete with canals, which opened to the public in 1907. Venice became an enclave of artists and writers, but by the 1950s had lost its luster. It doubled as a Mexican border town in Orson Welles's *Touch of Evil*. In succeeding decades, Venice drew artists and hippies. The city rebounded in the 1980s, but retains the image of a Bohemian beach community.

The industry started moving to Malibu in 1926 as part of the Malibu Beach Motion Picture Colony. Homeowners included Clara Bow, Ronald Colman, and Jack Warner. Filmmakers flocked to Malibu's picturesque beaches, including Paradise Cove (*Beach Blanket Bingo*), Point Dume (*Planet of the Apes*), Zuma (*Million Dollar Mermaid*), El Matador (*True Romance*), and Leo Carrillo (*Out of the Past*).

In 1913, Balboa Studios was established in Long Beach and made great use of the local scenery in a variety of films. Long Beach has achieved recognition as the home of the RMS *Queen Mary*, which is in dry dock and permanently in use as a hotel and tourist destination. The ship was constructed in 1936 and features an art deco design and elegant ballrooms and bars that have made it a popular film location in hundreds of films, including *The Poseidon Adventure* and *The Aviator*.

San Pedro has been a location manager's dream with such popular seaside destinations as Fort MacArthur (*A Few Good Men* and *Midway*), Cabrillo Beach Bathhouse (*Face/Off*), Sunken City (*The Big Lebowski*), Korean Friendship Bell (*The Usual Suspects*), Warner Grand Theatre (*Pearl Harbor*), Sixth Street (*Anchorman*), Walker's Café (*Gods and Monsters*), and Point Fermin (*500 Days of Summer*).

The mile-long Vincent Thomas Bridge, which links San Pedro to Terminal Island, has helped provide the perfect waterfront settings for crime thrillers such as *To Live and Die in L.A.* and the Nicolas Cage chase flick *Gone in Sixty Seconds*. Decades before the action films, Charlie Chaplin filmed scenes for *Modern Times* on Terminal Island.

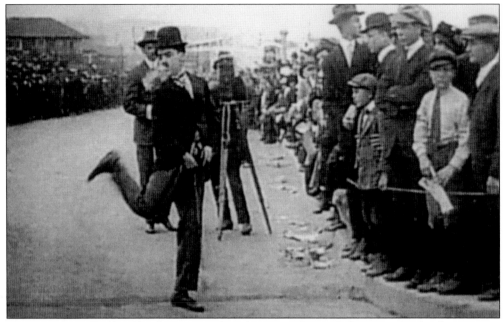

VENICE, 1914. Charlie Chaplin appeared as the iconic "tramp" character for the first time in *Kid Auto Races at Venice* (Mutual Film Corporation). Venice, California, was the first major resort attraction in the area when it opened in 1905, replicating Venice, Italy, with St. Mark's Square–style buildings and canals. It held the Junior Vanderbilt Cup Races on January 10, 1914. Chaplin filmed this scene on the northeast corner of Second Street (now Main Street) and Westminster Street in Venice.

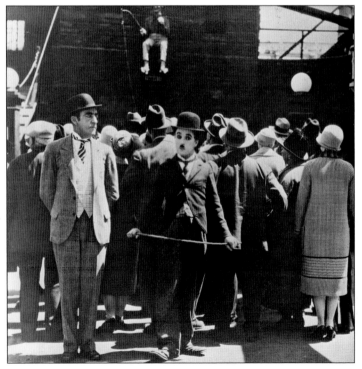

VENICE PIER, 1928. Charlie Chaplin in *The Circus* (United Artists) tries to lose a detective who thinks he is a pickpocket. He is standing in front of the 'Noah's Ark' fun house attraction at the pier (near Windward Avenue), demolished in 1946.

VENICE PIER, 1918.
Mack Sennett's
Bathing Beauties
Mary Thurman
and Vera Steadman
shoot a publicity
photograph
near the Venice
Pier advertising
Paramount Mack
Sennett Comedies.
Both Sennett and
Christie Comedies
employed Bathing
Beauties in the
films and for
publicity in general.

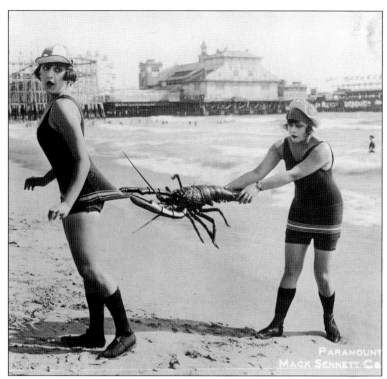

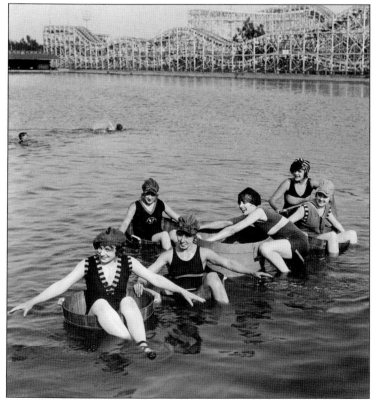

**VENICE LAGOON
1918.** Mack Sennett's
Bathing Beauties
frolic in the water at
the Venice Lagoon
(today's Venice Circle,
where Main Street
meets Windward
Avenue) publicizing
the Venice Tub Races,
which were filmed by
Sennett cameramen.
The Sennett shorts
introduced such
future stars as Gloria
Swanson and Carole
Lombard, who
appeared in short
films and represented
Sennett Comedies in
publicity stunts and
advertising films. In
the rear is the famous
"Race Thru the
Clouds" roller coaster
on the south side of
the Grand Lagoon.

61

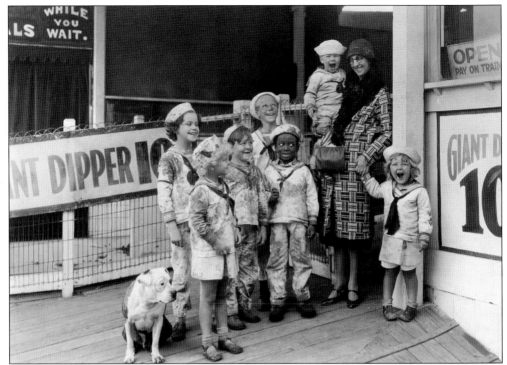

VENICE PIER, 1928. The members of Our Gang are covered in mud and causing mischief on the Venice Pier's Giant Dipper roller coaster in *Fair and Muddy* (Hal Roach Studios). This film is considered lost. In the group are Bobby "Wheezer" Hutchins, Jackie Condon, Jay R. Smith, Mildred Kornman, Harry Spear, Allen "Farina" Hoskins, Jean Darling, Bobby Dean, and Pete the Pup.

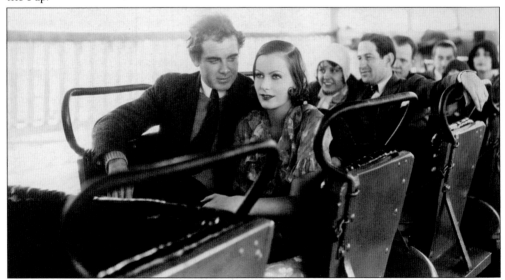

VENICE PIER, 1930. Greta Garbo and Charles Bickford in *Anna Christie* (MGM) ride the Some Kick roller coaster at the end of the Venice Pier. The pier's rides, doubling as the movie's Coney Island amusement park, were filmed on November 4, 1929. The Clarence Brown production was Garbo's first talkie.

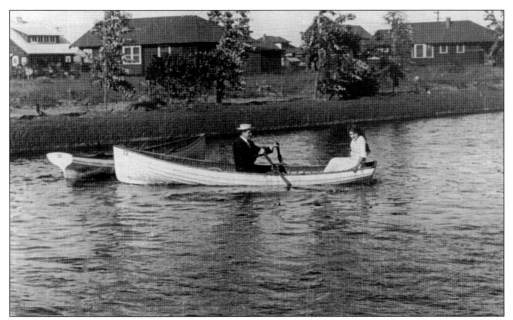

VENICE CANAL, 1910. D. W. Griffith brought his cast and crew out to Los Angeles to avoid the harsh East Coast winters starting in 1910. Here is a scene, reportedly shot at the five-year-old Venice canals for *Never Again* (Biograph), starring Mary Pickford. The Venice of America development opened in 1905 and became an instant attraction for tourists and filmmakers alike.

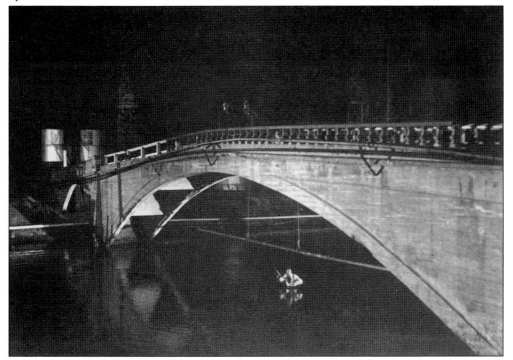

VENICE CANAL, 1958. Director-star Orson Welles made great use of the Venice canals in *Touch of Evil* (Universal). This bridge, spanning the Ballona Lagoon, was near the one-time Venice oil wells south of Washington Boulevard in today's Marina Peninsula.

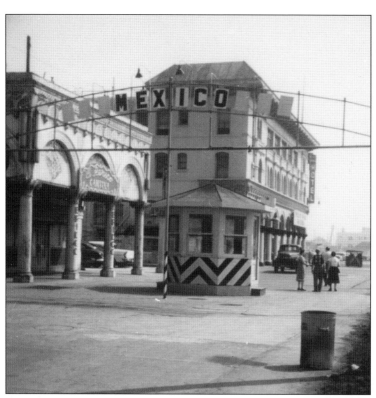

VENICE, 1958. Venice's Ocean Front Walk, just north of Windward Avenue, stands in for the Mexican border in *Touch of Evil* (Universal).

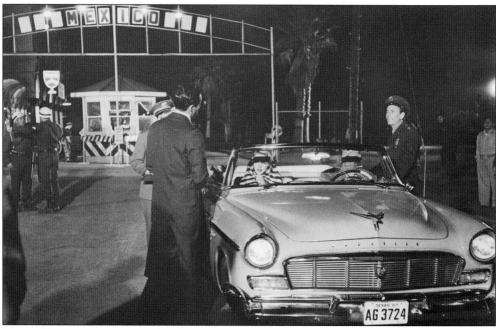

VENICE BOARDWALK, 1958. The classic single-take opening of *Touch of Evil* (Universal) follows this convertible from Pacific Avenue, down Windward Avenue, and onto the boardwalk. This film serves as a frozen-in-time historical record of Venice's landmarks during the beatnik era, showing many of the original buildings which have not survived.

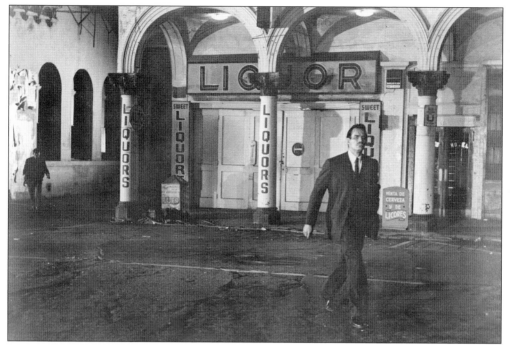

WINDWARD AVENUE, 1958. The St. Mark's Hotel annex (still standing) on Windward Avenue convincingly doubled as the seedy Ritz Hotel in *Touch of Evil* (Universal). Charlton Heston played a fearless Mexican narcotics officer.

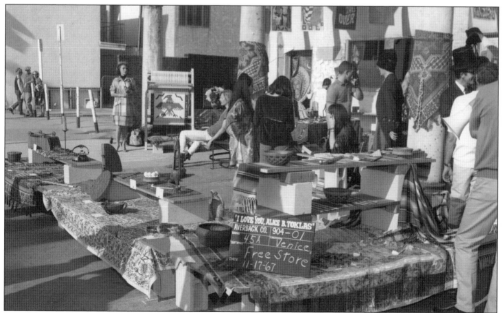

VENICE, 1968. The Peter Sellers counterculture comedy *I Love You, Alice B. Toklas* (Warner Bros.) staged a hippie bazaar at the site of today's Sidewalk Café. Assistant director Howard Kazanjian recalls frequently running out of food for the costumed hippie extras, as it was hard to tell them apart from the real Venice hippies living on the boardwalk. This outdoor setting was located at Windward Avenue in one of the original Venice of America columned buildings.

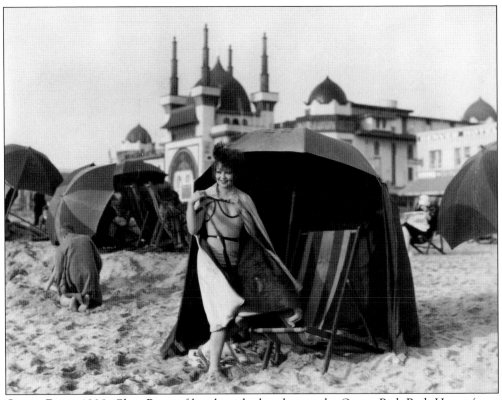

OCEAN PARK, 1928. Clara Bow is filmed on the beach near the Ocean Park Bath House (near Santa Monica) for a scene in *Red Hair* (Paramount). Made at the height of her fame, the film is now lost and only a fragment remains.

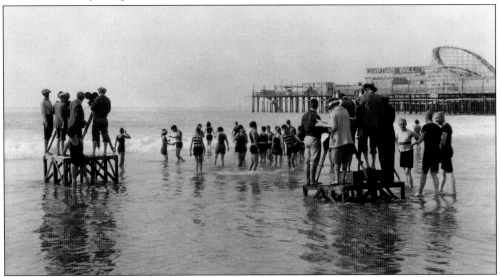

OCEAN PARK, 1926. The Santa Monica Beach has been used as a film location since 1909 when the first films were produced on the West Coast. Here a Film Booking Offices (FBO) studio production is being shot on the beach. Note the camera platforms for the camera units and the Ocean Park Pier in the background.

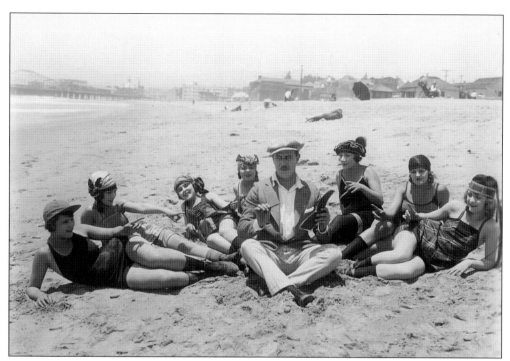

OCEAN PARK, 1919. Keystone star Ford Sterling and the Mack Sennett Bathing Beauties are seen here on the Santa Monica beach in a scene from *A Lady's Tailor* (Paramount). Note the Santa Monica Pier in the distant background, on the left.

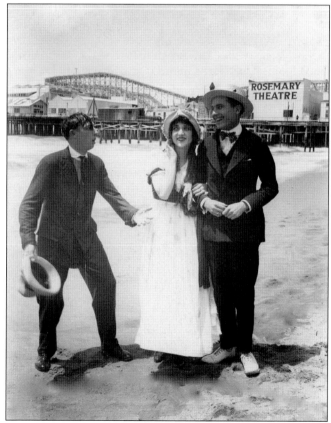

OCEAN PARK, 1915. Eddie Lyons, Victoria Forde, and Lee Moran, in *They Were On Their Honeymoon*, filmed in front of the Ocean Park Pier. Lyons and Moran were one of the early screen comedy duos and starred together with leading ladies like Forde for the Nestor/Christie Film Company under the Universal banner.

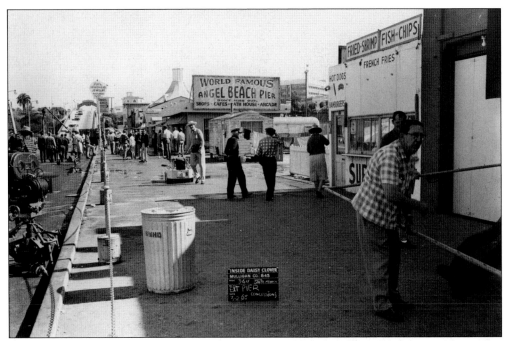

SANTA MONICA PIER SET PHOTOGRAPH, 1965. *Inside Daisy Clover* (Warner Bros.) filmed key scenes on the pier featuring Natalie Wood as a scruffy Angel Beach teenager with dreams of achieving stardom. The landmark served as the site of her character's seedy, ramshackle home. The pier has appeared in several period films, including *They Shoot Horses, Don't They?* and *Funny Girl*.

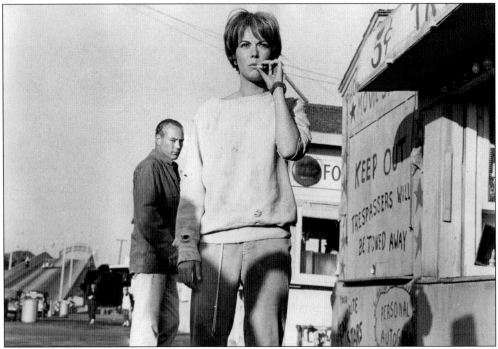

SANTA MONICA PIER, 1965. Natalie Wood starred in the film *Inside Daisy Clover* (Warner Bros.), along with Ruth Gordon, Christopher Plummer, Robert Redford, and Roddy McDowall.

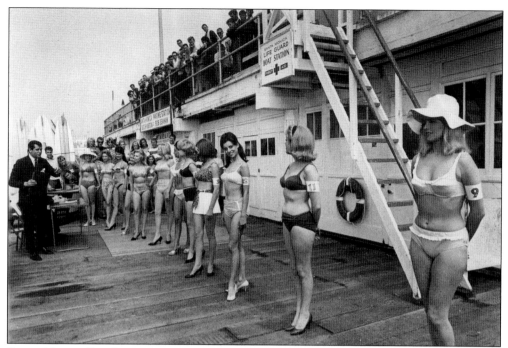

SANTA MONICA PIER LIFEGUARD STATION, 1965. Beauty contestants line up at the lifeguard station, once located on the pier's West end, in the beach party movie *Girls on the Beach* (Paramount). The film also featured The Beach Boys and Lesley Gore.

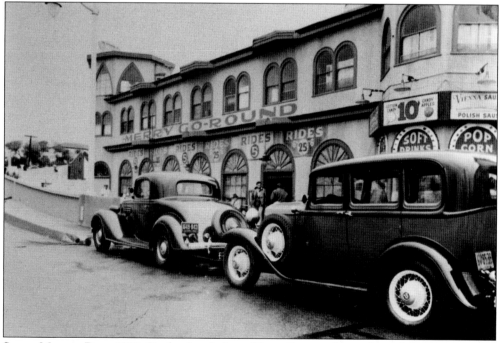

SANTA MONICA PIER, 1973. Production designer Henry Bumstead transformed the Santa Monica Pier to look like 1930s Chicago for *The Sting* (Universal). The old carousel building, which opened in 1916, was the center of attention in several scenes where Paul Newman is featured.

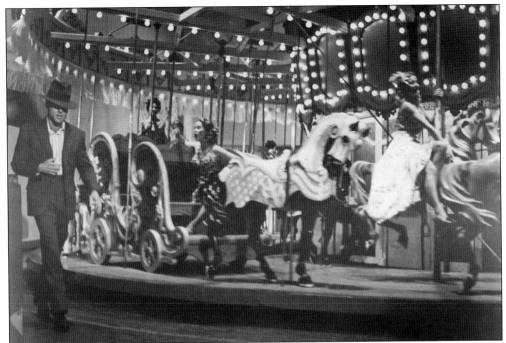

SANTA MONICA PIER CAROUSEL BUILDING, 1973. Robert Redford arrives in 1930s Chicago and strolls past the merry-go-round inside the carousel building, turned into a brothel/gambling parlor for George Roy Hill's *The Sting* (Universal).

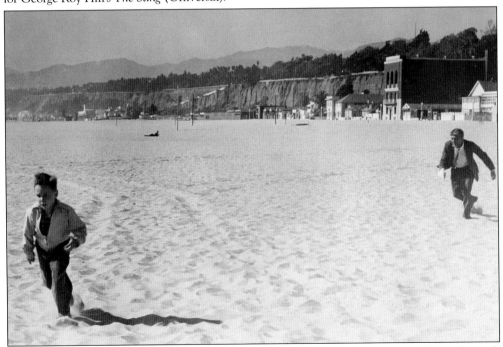

SANTA MONICA BEACH, 1957. Eduard Franz chases child actor Tim Hovey across the beach north of the Santa Monica Pier, with the Gold Coast homes and Palisades Park in the background, in a scene from the suspense thriller *Man Afraid* (Universal).

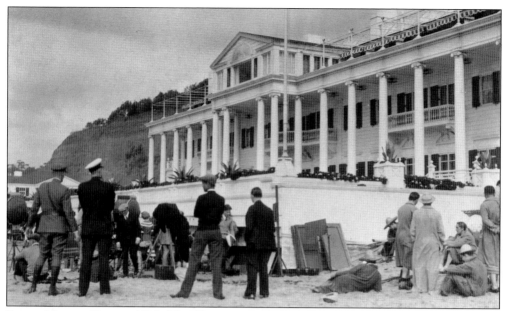

SANTA MONICA BEACH, 1930. The film crew prepares to shoot a scene with Marion Davies for *The Floradora Girl* (MGM) in front of her 118-room seaside retreat built by William Randolph Hearst. This colonial home was largely demolished in the 1950s with only the pool and guesthouse surviving. The remaining property, which was once featured as the Beverly Hills Beach Club on television's *Beverly Hills 90210*, is now open to the public as part of the Annenberg Community Beach House.

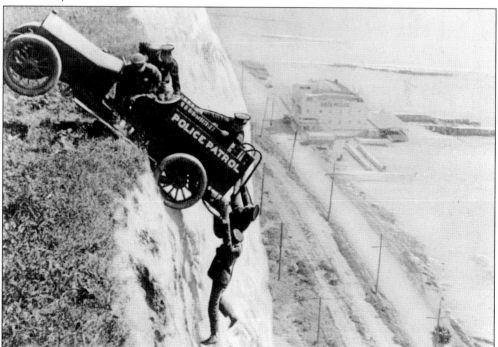

ABOVE PACIFIC COAST HIGHWAY, 1916. The Keystone Kops court disaster as their car hangs on the bluffs overlooking the Pacific Coast Highway.

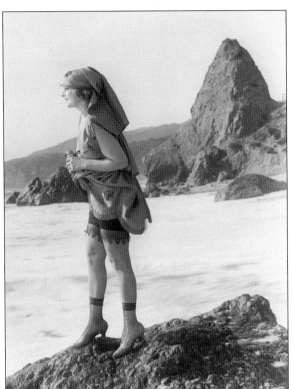

CASTLE ROCK—PACIFIC PALISADES, 1916. Mack Sennett Bathing Beauty Claire Anderson poses for a publicity photograph while standing on the beach near Castle Rock (just below the current location of the Getty Villa on Pacific Coast Highway). Some film historians believe that this beach may have provided the first California location to appear in a dramatic film (Selig's *Monte Cristo*, shot in 1907); others believe that beach may have been located in Laguna or La Jolla.

CASTLE ROCK—PACIFIC PALISADES, 1933. The crew sets up a shot for the Maureen O. Sullivan drama *Stage Mother* (MGM) on the beach along the Castellammare coast near Castle Rock. These days, the rock is no longer recognizable as it was leveled to accommodate the widening of the highway. This beach was also a filming location for Charlie Chaplin's popular 1917 comedy short *The Adventurer*.

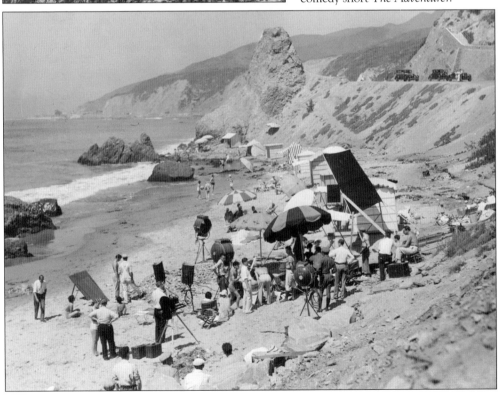

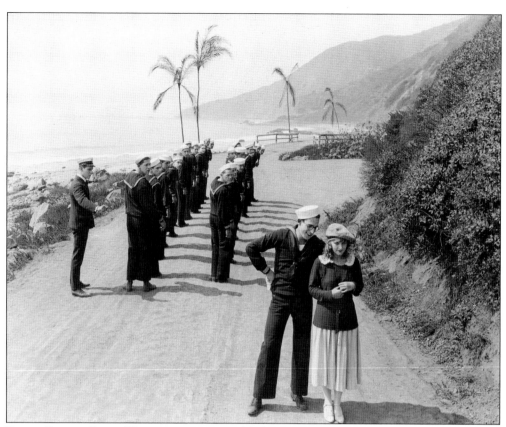

BESIDE PACIFIC COAST HIGHWAY, 1921. Harold Lloyd romances Mildred Davis in the mythical port of Khairpura-Bhandanna in *A Sailor-Made Man* (Hal Roach Studios), Lloyd's first feature-length film. This view, facing northwest, of the Santa Monica Mountains can be seen from the Topanga Beach area.

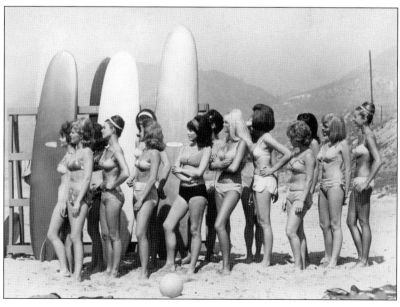

CORRAL BEACH, 1965. The sixth installment of the *Beach Party* series, *How to Stuff a Wild Bikini* (AIP), was partially shot at Malibu's Corral Beach, also known as Dan Blocker Beach.

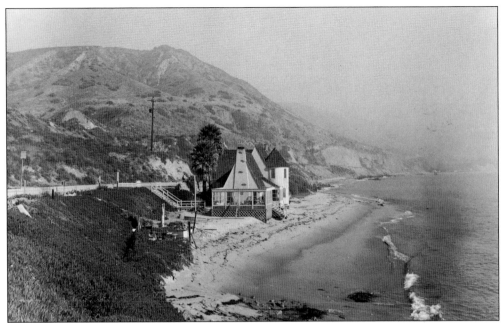

MALIBU, 1945. This beach house on Latigo Shore Drive, near today's Beaurivage Restaurant, was the setting for murder and deception in *Mildred Pierce* (Warner Bros.), starring Joan Crawford and Zachary Scott. This home was one of many built by the Rindge family, owners of the original Rancho Malibu, but was destroyed by a storm in the 1960s.

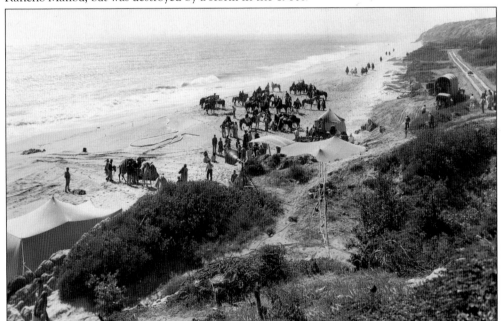

LEO CARRILLO STATE BEACH, 1946. Once known as Sequit Beach, this favorite spot was transformed into an Arab chieftain's secret encampment for the Yvonne De Carlo costumer *Slave Girl* (Universal). Carrillo Beach appears in the opening sequences of *Beach Blanket Bingo* and *Grease* and serves as Ralph Macchio's seaside hangout in *The Karate Kid* and the black sand beach in Clint Eastwood's *Letters from Iwo Jima*.

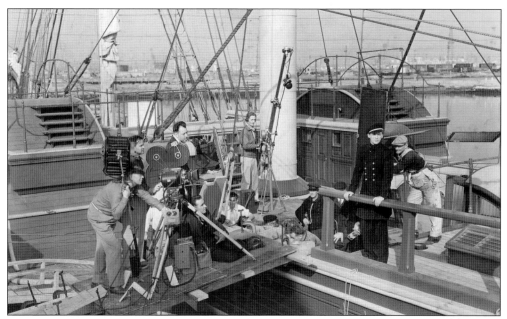

SAN PEDRO—PORT OF LOS ANGELES, 1939. Douglas Fairbanks Jr. and crew film a scene for *Rulers of the Sea* (Paramount) on a ship named *Dog Star*, which was an exact replica for the first successful transatlantic paddle steamer. The film's director, Frank Lloyd (*Mutiny on the Bounty*), is seated below the camera filming Douglas Fairbanks Jr. Other locations used by the production company included San Miguel Island, Catalina Island, and Wilmington, California.

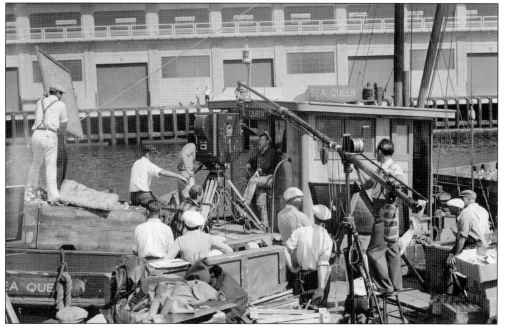

SAN PEDRO—PORT OF LOS ANGELES 1933. Film crews set up a shot for *Hell or High Water* (Paramount), starring Richard Arlen, who can be seen in front of the wheelhouse before the camera. The location was the Berth 60 warehouse building adjacent to the Los Angeles Municipal Warehouse in the Harbor Foreign Trade Zone No. 4.

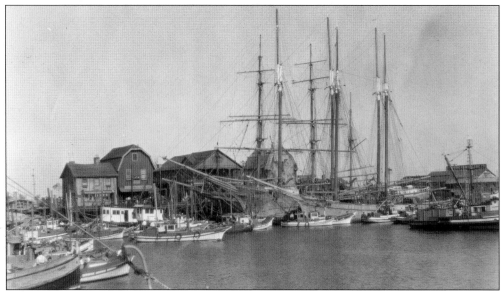

SAN PEDRO, 1930. Located only 20 miles from the heart of downtown Los Angeles, San Pedro Harbor doubles as a quaint New England–style fishing village in *Min and Bill* (MGM), starring Marie Dressler and Wallace Beery. The MGM studio set dressing department modified the fishing village for filming and brought in a couple of 19th-century sailing ships for added atmosphere.

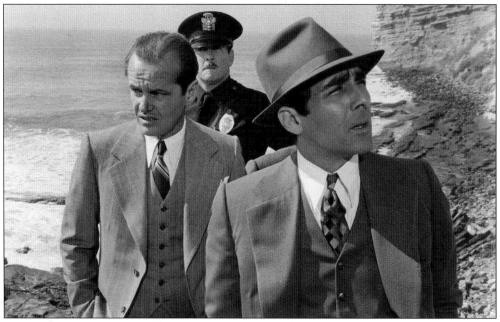

SAN PEDRO—"SUNKEN CITY," 1974. *Chinatown's* J. J. Gittes (Jack Nicholson) brings Lieutenant Escobar (Perry Lopez) to an isolated water run-off location at "Sunken City," a strange series of eroded cliffs at the southern end of San Pedro's Point Fermin Park. As late as 1929, homes stood on these cliffs before sliding into the sea. All that is left today is a windy sandlot with tilting foundations, cracked pieces of sidewalk, and a sensational view. Sunken City is also seen in *The Big Lebowski*, where Walter (John Goodman) eulogizes surfer Donny while an ocean breeze blows his ashes back onto The Dude's (Jeff Bridges) face.

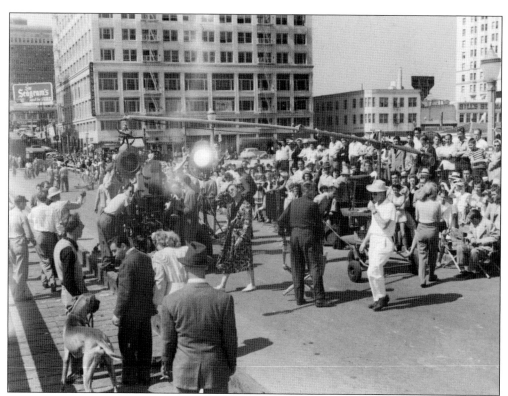

Long Beach, 1947. Long Beach stands in for Florida in *Fun on a Weekend* (United Artists), starring Eddie Bracken (center in bathrobe), seen here at the intersection of South Pine Avenue and Seaside Boulevard (now Seaside Way).

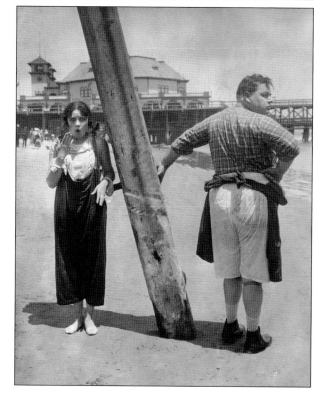

Long Beach Pike, 1918. Roscoe "Fatty" Arbuckle and Alice Lake film a scene on the beach adjacent to the Pike Amusement pier in Long Beach for *The Cook* (Paramount). Roscoe Arbuckle's Comique Studio was located in Long Beach, California, at this time.

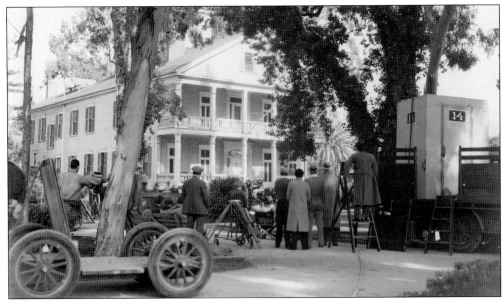

WILMINGTON, 1930. Gary Cooper and Mary Brian star in the Civil War love story *Only the Brave* (Paramount). The crew shot several scenes at the Greek Revival–style Banning House, which was built in San Pedro–adjacent Wilmington in 1864 by Gen. Phineas Banning and donated to the City of Los Angeles in 1927. Studio location departments listed the Banning House as a location when a film's setting needed a Southern plantation–style house and grounds. The 23-room mansion and 20-acre park grounds were also used for the Paramount production *Hula*, starring Clara Bow, in 1927.

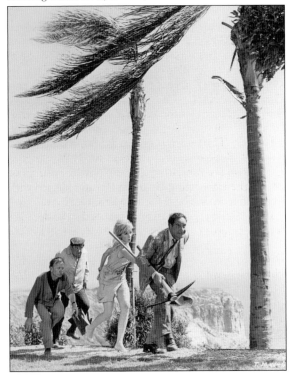

PALOS VERDES PENINSULA, 1963. North of San Pedro, Palos Verdes's Portuguese Point is home to the tilting palm trees that form a "W" in *It's a Mad Mad Mad Mad World* (United Artists). Two of the palms still exist on private PV property, but they can be viewed from public land near the top of the point. Mickey Rooney, Buddy Hackett, Dorothy Provine, and Sid Caesar discover the site of the buried money under the "W" palm tree site.

Four

THE WESTSIDE AND CULVER CITY

COLLEGE TOWN, COMPANY TOWN

West Los Angeles encompasses Bel-Air, Holmby Hills, Brentwood, Century City, Westwood, and Cheviot Hills. Culver City, which developed into a studio hub dominated by Metro-Goldwyn-Mayer, lies to the south-southeast of these areas.

Numerous icons from Hollywood's golden age resided on the Westside, including Claudette Colbert, Lauren Bacall and Humphrey Bogart, Joan Crawford, Lana Turner, Shirley Temple, Marilyn Monroe, and Judy Garland.

A great glimpse of the Westside's golden age can be found in the 1960 Kirk Douglas-Kim Novak drama, *Strangers When We Meet*, filmed along Sunset Boulevard, Kenter Canyon, and Barrington Court. Westwood includes UCLA, a favorite film backdrop, and Century City primarily consists of large high-rise buildings constructed on the former backlot of Twentieth Century-Fox. Its futuristic look was used to great effect in *Conquest of the Planet of the Apes*, and the Fox Tower was immortalized on screen as Nakatomi Plaza in *Die Hard*.

Even though the amorphous "Hollywood" often receives the credit, Culver City deserves recognition for the many classics produced during the industry's golden age. Developer Harry N. Culver courted film companies with free land in 1915. Thomas H. Ince seized the opportunity and founded Triangle Films with D. W. Griffith and Mack Sennett on 16 acres at 10202 Washington Boulevard. In 1919, Samuel Goldwyn bought the studio, inheriting a superb physical plant, but was pushed out of his own company. In 1924, his then struggling Goldwyn Pictures merged with failing Metro Pictures and tiny Louis B. Mayer Productions. The resulting Metro-Goldwyn-Mayer became the most profitable film plant in the world within three years and remained so for decades. The studio is now the home of the Sony Pictures Entertainment, and Culver City is still known as the "Heart of Screenland."

Ince established his next studio at 9336 Washington Boulevard in 1919. Its white colonial facade became one of the most recognizable in Hollywood history. After Ince's death in 1924, the studio became the production headquarters for Cecil B. DeMille, RKO Radio Pictures, David O. Selznick, and Desilu Productions. Now named Culver Studios, today it is a rental facility.

Hal Roach also built a studio in Culver City, standing from 1920 to 1963, at the southwest corner of Washington and National Boulevards. Since demolished, it is commemorated by a plaque as the "Laugh Factory to the World."

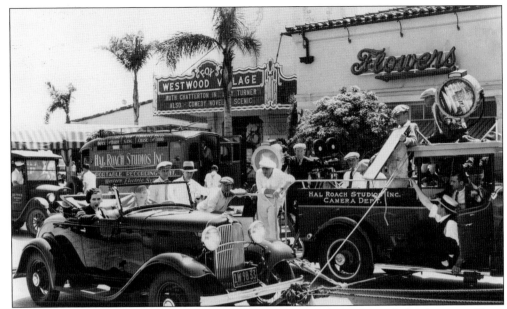

WESTWOOD VILLAGE, 1933. Patsy Kelly, Thelma Todd, and the Hal Roach Studios crew film a scene in front of the new Fox Village Theatre for *Beauty and the Bus* (MGM). Built in 1931 at the corner of Broxton and Weyburn Avenues, the Village Theatre is often host to lavish movie premieres. For *Beauty and the Bus*, a rare 1933 Chrysler Roadster was featured as the car the girls won in a raffle. Shooting was predominately done in the Westwood area where they staged car chases, crashes, and stunts on streets that were empty since much of the development of Westwood was just beginning.

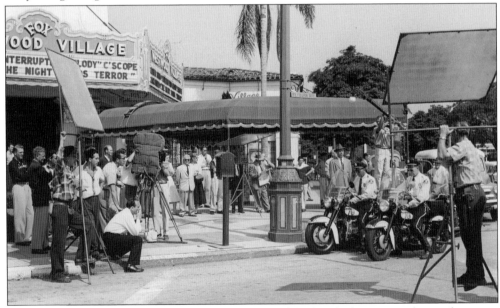

WESTWOOD VILLAGE, 1956. Director Alex Segal, crouching beside the camera, directs the action in the suspense drama *Ransom* (Universal), starring Glenn Ford and Donna Reed. The Fox Village Theatre is the background for this scene featuring two Los Angeles motorcycle police officers parked at the intersection of Weyburn and Broxton Avenues.

WESTWOOD VILLAGE, 1957.
Troubled UCLA student
James MacArthur starts a
fistfight at the Bruin Theatre
and discovers a parking
ticket on his car in *The Young
Stranger* (RKO). This was
the first film of *Manchurian
Candidate* director John
Frankenheimer and was
shot at several Westwood
Village area locations.

WESTWOOD VILLAGE, 1943.
Designed by S. Charles Lee
in 1937 and named after
the UCLA mascot, the
Bruin Theatre provides a
matte shot background for
the 1944 romantic comedy
Janie (Warner Bros.). Note
the 1929 Holmby Hall clock
tower in the background
on the right. The setting is
a small American town by
the name of Hortonville,
where a teenage girl lives
near a military base.

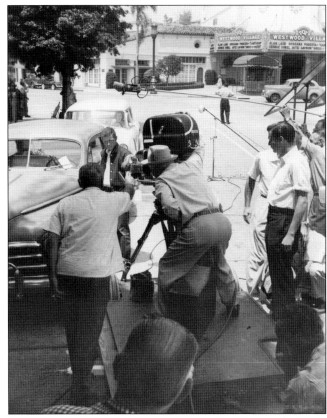

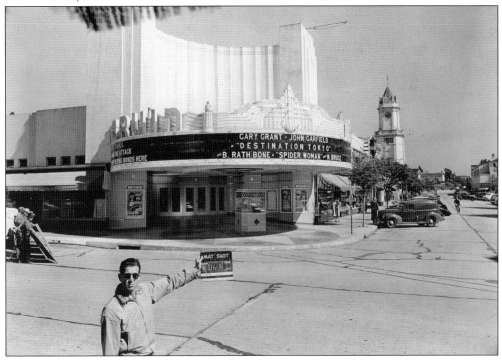

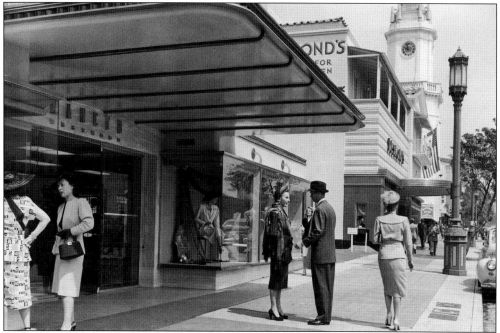

WESTWOOD VILLAGE, 1948. Franchot Tone stars as a private detective tailing a mysterious wife played by Lynn Merrick in *I Love Trouble* (Columbia) in Westwood Village. Here are Tone and Merrick standing in front of Nancy's of Westwood women's department store on Westwood Boulevard. Other locations in Westwood Village included the Janss Real Estate office at Broxton and Kinross Avenues.

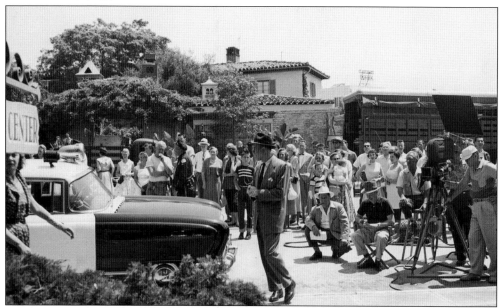

WESTWOOD VILLAGE, 1955. A crowd gathers as the cast and crew film a scene for the film noir *No Man's Woman* (Republic) on Kinross Avenue a half a block east of Westwood Boulevard. The film stars Marie Windsor and John Archer and used numerous local buildings, including the El Encanto Building at 1129 Glendon Avenue.

a scene at an apartment in Westwood Village for *The Accused* (Paramount). Most of the apartment houses in the Westwood area were of the Spanish Mediterranean style with tiled stairs and red tile roofs. Studio location departments noted the Westwood area as one of the more popular location sites in Los Angeles.

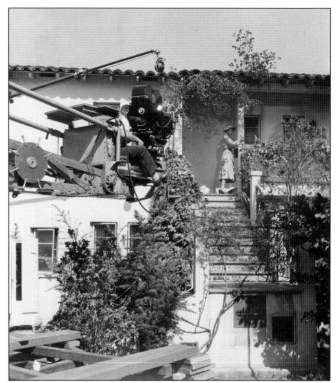

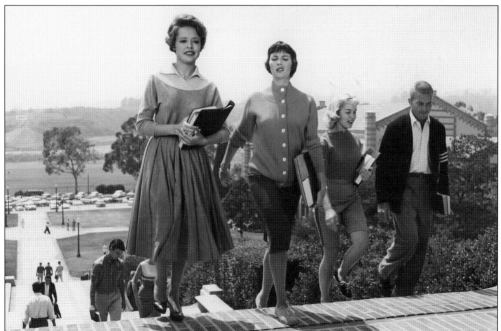

UCLA, 1958. Jill Corey and Barbara Bostock walk to the classroom for final exams in the musical *Senior Prom* (Columbia), in which UCLA played a typical American university. Kaufman Hall (formerly the women's gymnasium and dance building) can be seen in the background from the top of the Janss Steps.

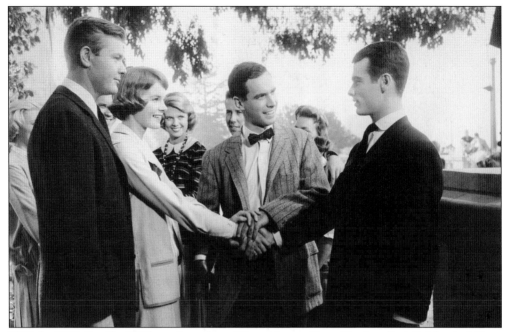

UCLA, 1959. Bradford Dillman introduces Diane Varsi to Dean Stockwell while Martin Milner looks on in the crime thriller *Compulsion* (Twentieth Century-Fox), directed by Richard Fleischer. Various UCLA locations such as Royce Hall, Janss Steps, and other classroom buildings were used in the film.

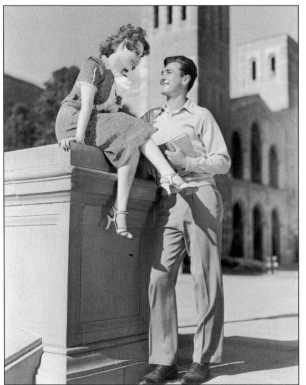

UCLA, 1938. Famed college basketball star Hank Luisetti (playing himself) stands with actress Eleanor Whitney at the top of Janss Steps for a publicity photograph during the filming of *Campus Confessions* (Paramount). Betty Grable starred in this story about a college basketball team. Royce Hall (in the background) dominated the original quad area, where many films and television shows have been shot.

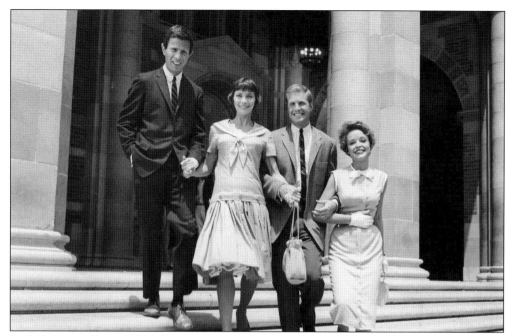

UCLA Royce Hall, 1958. Future television producer Jimmy Komack, Barbara Bostock, Paul Hampton, and Jill Corey walk the steps at UCLA's Royce Hall in *Senior Prom* (Columbia). The film is a campus musical with musical star cameos by Louis Prima, Keely Smith, Bob Crosby, Mitch Miller, and Freddie Martin and his orchestra.

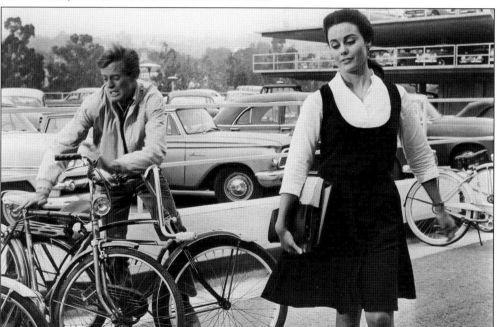

UCLA Campus, 1964. Five years before *Easy Rider*, Peter Fonda has bike trouble at the Royce Hall parking lot, much to the amusement of Sharon Hugueny in *The Young Lovers* (MGM). The film is a controversial drama about forbidden love and pregnancy. The production used the UCLA campus and Westwood locations for the story's backdrop.

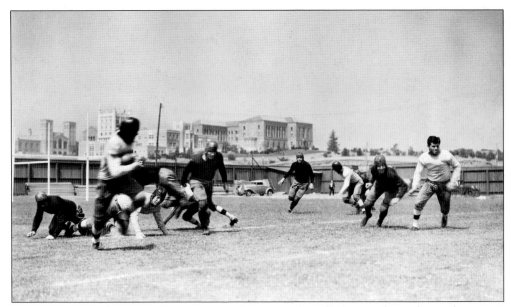

UCLA Campus, 1932. The murder mystery *70,000 Witnesses* (Paramount) was shot at the UCLA campus and starred Dorothy Jordan and Johnny Mack Brown. The plot revolves around a college football player who is killed during the big game in front of the titular crowd of sports fans. Royce, Kerckhoff, and Moore Halls can be seen in the background.

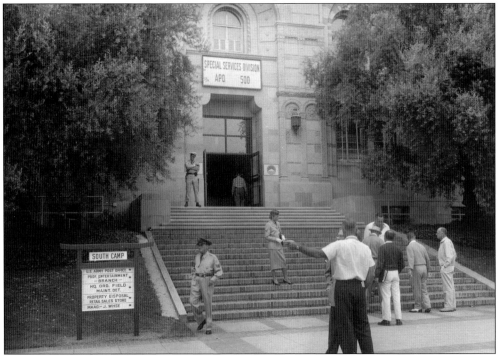

UCLA Kinsey Hall, 1958. Frank Tashlin's *The Geisha Boy* (Paramount), starring Jerry Lewis, featured the Humanities Building (formerly Kinsey Hall) as a U.S. military outpost in Japan. A prop army sign covers a chiseled-in-stone entryway quotation from Psalm 119, which might have looked out of place for the Asian setting.

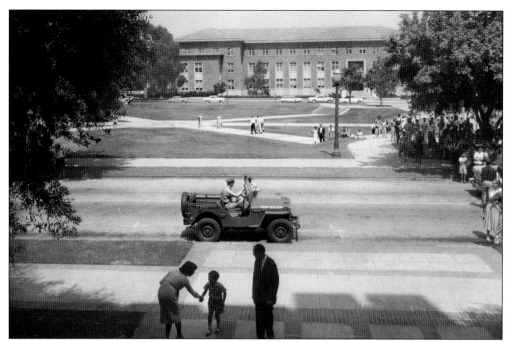

UCLA CAMPUS, 1958. Dickson Court South, looking east towards Murphy Hall, provides a Japanese background for *The Geisha Boy* (Paramount), starring Jerry Lewis and Suzanne Pleshette.

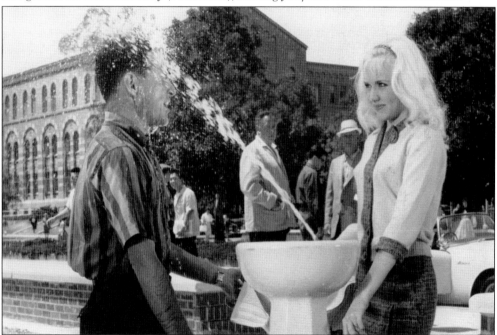

UCLA CAMPUS, 1962. Two cast members try out the drinking fountain special effects while director Frank Tashlin watches. The action takes place in front of Haines Hall for the campus comedy *Bachelor Flat* (Twentieth Century-Fox). Other movies partially shot at UCLA include the Eddie Murphy *Nutty Professor* remake, *National Lampoon's Van Wilder, Angels and Demons,* and *Old School.*

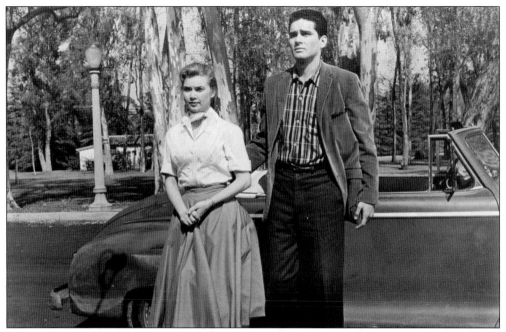

HOLMBY PARK, 1958. B-movie starlet Yvonne Lime is set on a path of delinquency and depravity in the exploitation film *High School Hellcats* (AIP), costarring Bret Halsey. The action takes place on Comstock Avenue with Holmby Park in the background.

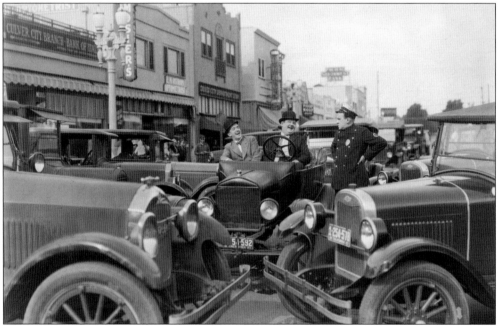

CULVER CITY, 1927. Laurel and Hardy film a scene for *Leave 'Em Laughing* on Main Street just north of its intersection with Culver Boulevard. Main Street was used as a background for many films made by the various studios based in Culver City, including Ince, Goldwyn, MGM, DeMille, Pathé, RKO/Pathé, Selznick, and Hal Roach. Many of the same buildings exist to this day on Main Street and are still being used by film companies as a backdrop.

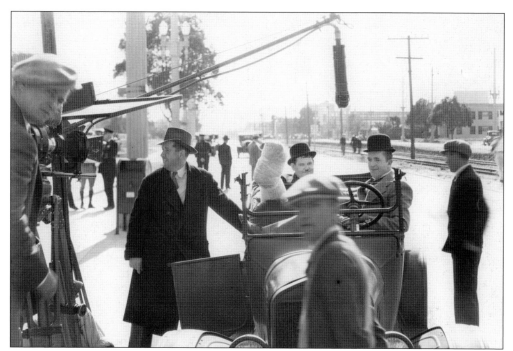

CULVER CITY, 1932. Laurel and Hardy and crew prepare for a scene in front of Culver City Hall (9770 Culver Boulevard), used as a key location in two of their films. It first doubled as a hospital for the film *Country Hospital* in 1932 and served as the Hall of Justice in *Going Bye-Bye* in 1934.

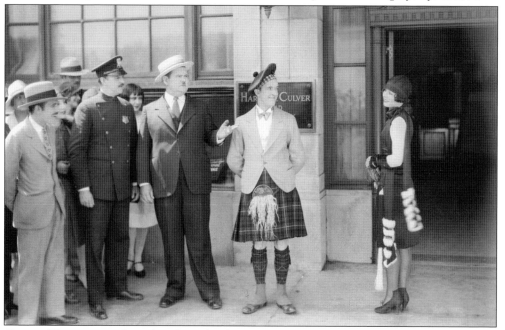

CULVER HOTEL, 1927. Laurel and Hardy film a scene from *Putting Pants on Philip* in front of the Culver Hotel (9400 Culver Boulevard) in downtown Culver City. In 1939, the munchkin cast of *The Wizard of Oz* stayed in the hotel, which is conveniently located down the street from the old MGM studio.

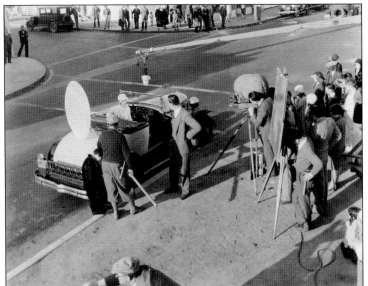

VENICE BOULEVARD AND MAIN STREET, 1930. Director Sam Wood and crew film a scene for *The Sins of the Children* (MGM), starring Robert Montgomery and Leila Hyams, near the intersection of Venice Boulevard, Bagley Avenue, and Main Street.

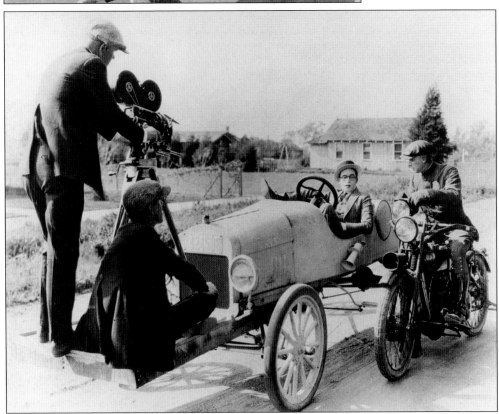

PALMS, 1922. Harold Lloyd films a scene for *Dr. Jack* in Palms, a residential community adjacent to Culver City. Cameraman Walter Lundin stands on the mounted platform with director Fred Newmeyer seated beside him. Note the wooden platform attached to the front of the car. There was only enough room on the platform for a cameraman and a director without any safety restraints, so they kept the speed of the car to a minimum to avoid any accidents.

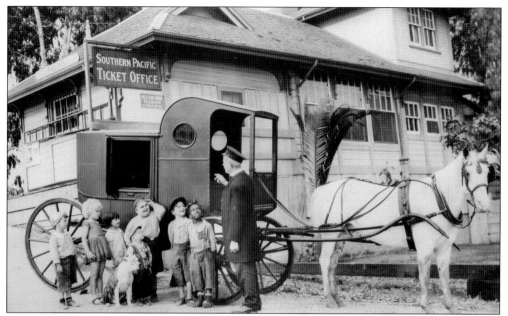

PALMS, 1928. Our Gang listens to character actor Richard Cummings in a scene from *Old Gray Hoss* (Roach/MGM) at the Palms Railway Depot. The Our Gang group includes Jean Darling, Mary Ann Jackson, Pete the Dog, Bobby "Wheezer" Hutchins, Joe Cobb, Harry Spear, and Allen "Farina" Hoskins. This depot in Palms, the oldest city (1886) to be annexed to the city of Los Angeles (1915), often appeared in the movies as a rural train station.

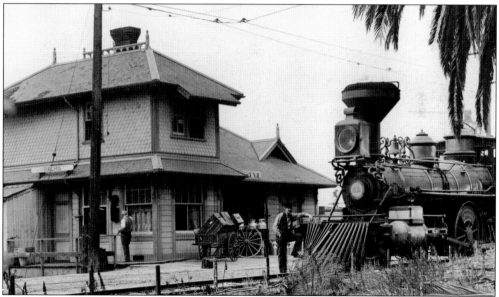

PALMS, 1939. This photograph of the Palms depot was taken by the MGM location department in September 1939, when the station was no longer in use. Located near Exposition and National Boulevards, the station was prepped for the film *Bad Little Angel*, starring Virginia Weidler and Gene Reynolds. The 19th-century locomotive in the photograph was Engine No. 22, used in countless films well into the 1950s. The building was moved in the 1970s to Heritage Square Museum, near the Pasadena Freeway, where it still stands today.

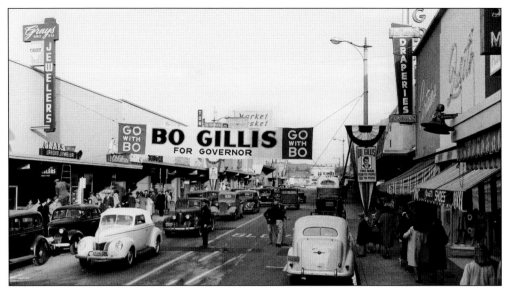

CULVER CITY, 1961. MGM Studio used the newly opened Culver Center shopping district for the political drama *Ada*, starring Dean Martin as gubernatorial candidate Bo Gillis and Susan Hayward as his supportive wife, Ada. The film took place in a small town in the Deep South, despite the telltale L.A.–based signage for "Culver Center Drugs" (above the "Bo Gillis" banner and below the "Market Basket" sign in the middle of the photograph). The shopping district, located near the intersection of Venice Boulevard and Overland Avenue, has been completely rebuilt and is almost unrecognizable today.

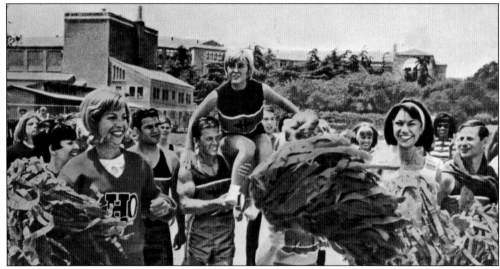

UNIVERSITY HIGH SCHOOL, 1965. This West Los Angeles school, named for its proximity to UCLA, played a prominent role in the track-team comedy *Billie* (United Artists), starring Patty Duke as a teenage tomboy. The campus has also been featured in Roger Vadim's *Pretty Maids All in a Row*, *Bruce Almighty*, *Valentine's Day* (where Taylor Swift and Taylor Lautner kiss for the cameras), and the Judd Apatow productions *Pineapple Express* (where Seth Rogen picks up Amber Heard) and *Drillbit Taylor* (where Owen Wilson teaches the bullies a lesson). Other frequently filmed Westside high schools include Hamilton (*Bye Bye Birdie*), Santa Monica (*Rebel Without a Cause*), Palisades (*Carrie*), and Venice (*Grease*).

Five

BEVERLY HILLS AND MID-WILSHIRE
MANSIONS AND CITYSCAPES

The glamorous image of Beverly Hills was cemented in 1920 when newlywed superstars Douglas Fairbanks and Mary Pickford moved into a remodeled hunting lodge in Beverly Hills, which the press dubbed "Pickfair." Their power, wealth, and elegance captured the imagination of film fans all over the world. Other stars and moguls followed suit, and soon Beverly Hills real estate became highly sought after. With its tree-lined streets and sprawling estates, Beverly Hills also made a great film location.

Early film credits include Douglas Fairbanks in *He Comes Up Smiling* (1918) and Charlie Chaplin in *The Idle Class* (1921). The Beverly Hills Speedway appeared in *The Roaring Road* in 1919. Local homes convincingly doubled for European estates. Other famous locations include the Beverly Wilshire Hotel (*Pretty Woman*), Beverly Hills Hotel (*The Bad and the Beautiful*), Rodeo Drive (*American Gigolo*), Beverly Hills City Hall (*In a Lonely Place*), and the Greystone Mansion (*There Will Be Blood*).

Wilshire Boulevard cuts east-west through the center of Los Angeles and Beverly Hills, running 16 miles from downtown to the Pacific Ocean in Santa Monica. Mid-Wilshire includes many diverse neighborhoods, including Koreatown and Hancock Park. Mid-Wilshire also includes the "Miracle Mile," which is a strip of stunning art deco buildings and other architectural treasures.

Hancock Park is one of the most lavishly appointed neighborhoods, established in the 1920s, featuring historical homes and impeccably manicured lawns. Perhaps the most famous home in the area was the Cunningham house in the sitcom *Happy Days*, located on North Cahuenga Avenue. The design of the house easily allowed it to pass for Milwaukee, Wisconsin, where the series was set. It was previously the home of Mexican spitfire Lupe Velez in the 1930s.

Another famous location in the area was the Getty Mansion at the northwest corner of Wilshire and Irving, which appeared in *Sunset Boulevard* and *Rebel Without a Cause*. The house was demolished, and the site is now home to an office building.

Mid-Wilshire and Hancock Park made desirable neighborhoods for celebrities, such as Nat King Cole, Howard Hughes, and Mae West. A row of museums also populates the area, including the Los Angeles County Museum of Art and the Petersen Automotive Museum.

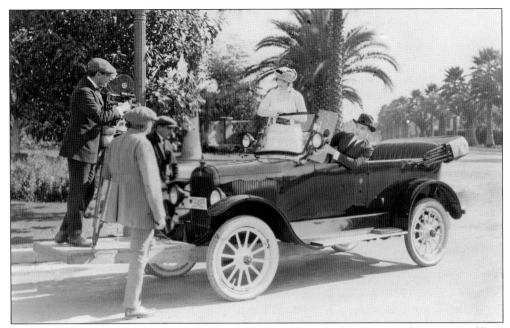

BEVERLY DRIVE AND SUNSET BOULEVARD, 1920. Stars Douglas MacLean and Doris May film a scene for *What's Your Husband Doing* (Ince) on location at the intersection of Beverly and Crescent Drives and Sunset Boulevard.

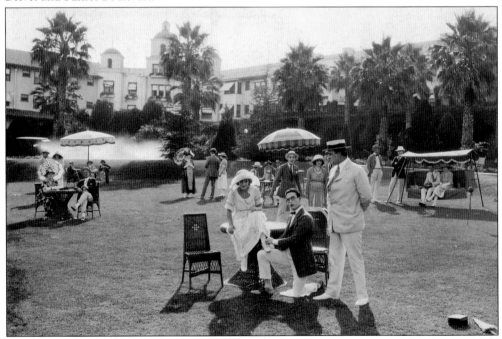

THE BEVERLY HILLS HOTEL, 1921. Spoiled idler Harold Lloyd courts heiress Mildred Davis while her father looks on in *A Sailor-Made Man* (Roach). The hotel plays the Abingdon Arms, an ultra-fashionable summer resort overlooking the bluffs (actually Santa Monica's Palisades Park, nearly 10 miles away). Lloyd liked Beverly Hills so much that he later purchased land above the Beverly Hills Hotel to build his own famous Green Acres estate.

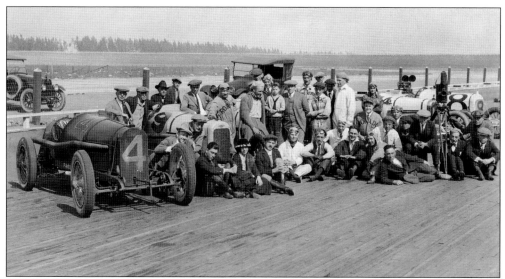

BEVERLY DRIVE, 1921. Wallace Reid poses with the cast and crew at the Beverly Speedway at South Beverly Drive and Wilshire Boulevard, where they filmed scenes for *The Roaring Road* (Paramount). This film helped to popularize the racing film genre and was followed by *Excuse My Dust*. The racetrack was eventually moved to Culver City, and then the South Beverly Drive area was developed into a residential area south of Wilshire into the 1930s.

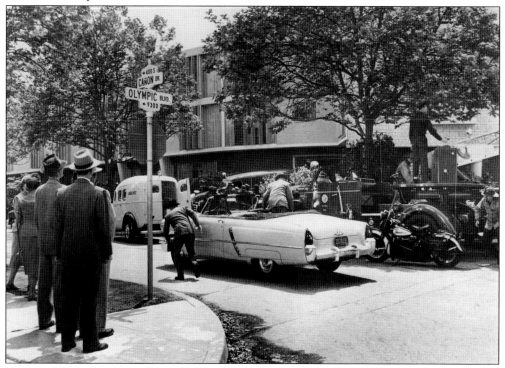

OLYMPIC BOULEVARD AND CANON DRIVE, 1952. The cast and crew prepare a scene at the Beverly Carlton Hotel for *My Pal Gus* (Twentieth Century-Fox). Located at 9400 West Olympic Boulevard, the Beverly Carlton (today known as the Avalon Hotel) was a celebrity haunt where Marilyn Monroe lived for a period of time.

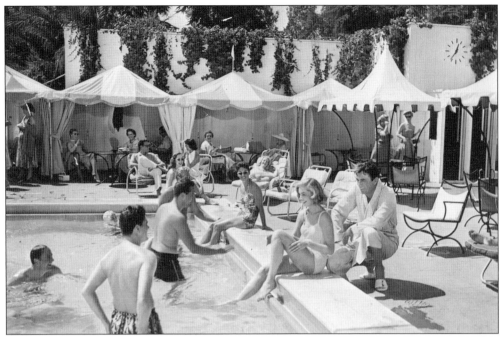

THE BEVERLY HILLS HOTEL POOL, 1957. The famed pool has been the location of numerous films throughout the years, including Vincente Minnelli's *Designing Woman* (MGM), starring Gregory Peck and Lauren Bacall (seen at right). The Beverly Hills Hotel pool has been a popular place, where agents, actors, producers, and other celebrities have gathered since it was built in 1934.

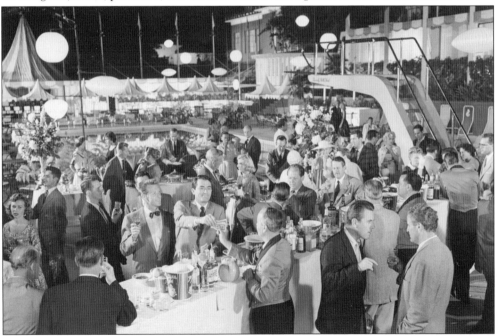

THE BEVERLY HILLS HOTEL, 1957. A party scene is filmed around the pool for *Designing Woman* (MGM). Gregory Peck is seen in the center of the photograph giving money to the bartender. Other films shot at the hotel include *The Bad and the Beautiful*, *Shampoo*, and *California Suite*.

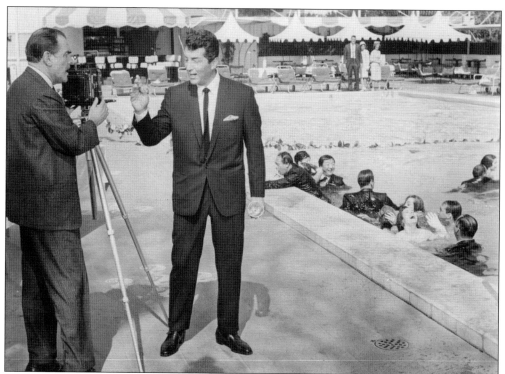

THE BEVERLY HILLS HOTEL, 1963. Mischievous playboy Dean Martin pushes fellow cast members into the pool in the comedy *Who's Been Sleeping in My Bed?* (Paramount), costarring Elizabeth Montgomery and Carol Burnett (in her first film role).

J. W. ROBINSON'S, 1957. Aldo Ray helps model Anne Bancroft escape killers at a J. W. Robinson's fashion show across from the Beverly Hilton in Jacques Tourneur's film noir *Nightfall* (Columbia). The Beverly Hills branch of Robinsons opened in 1952 and was a glamorous store where many celebrities shopped. The outdoor courtyard of the store was the site of fashion shows and was used as a film location several times over the years.

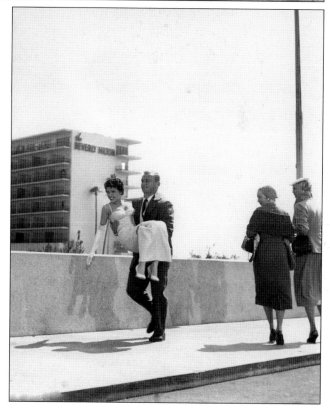

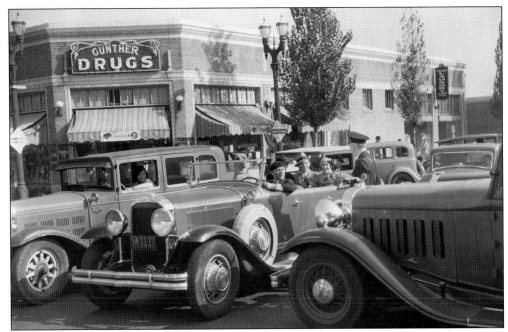

BEVERLY HILLS, 1934. Gracie Allen, George Burns, and Charles Ruggles are stopped by the police in a scene from *Six of a Kind* (Paramount), filmed at the corner of Rodeo Drive and South Santa Monica Boulevard. Note Gunther Drugs in the background; it was the first drugstore in Beverly Hills.

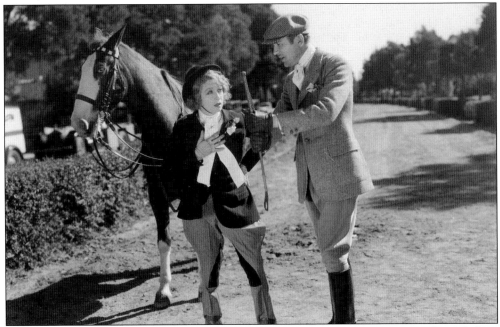

RODEO DRIVE, 1932. June Clyde and John Roche stand in the Rodeo Drive Bridle Path for a scene in the comedy *Cohens and Kellys in Hollywood* (Universal). Beverly Hills was the only city in Los Angeles that had a bridle path for residents who owned horses. It was installed in 1924 and became a Beverly Hills attraction until it was removed in the late 1950s.

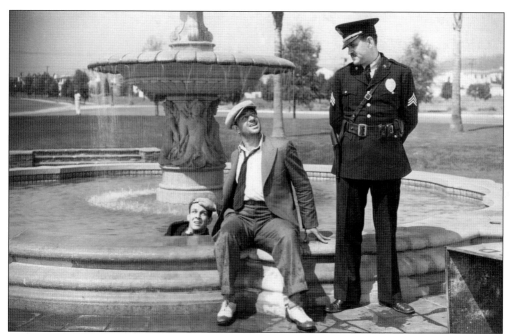

DOHENY PARK, 1931. T. Roy Barnes and Monty Collins film a scene in the fountain at Doheny Park, located at Doheny Drive and Santa Monica Boulevard in Beverly Hills, for *Once A Hero* (Mermaid Comedies). Doheny Park was the east end of Beverly Park, a long strip of parkland that followed Santa Monica Boulevard to the west, ending at Whittier Drive.

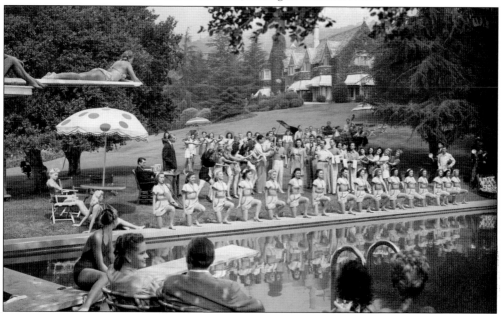

LEWIS ESTATE, 1946. A female dance troupe lines up poolside at the estate of banker George Lewis, used for *Night and Day* (Warner Bros.), starring Cary Grant as a fictionalized version of composer Cole Porter. The Lewis estate was located in the hills between Benedict Canyon and Coldwater Canyon. Many films from the late 1920s were made at the English-style baronial mansion and on the grounds.

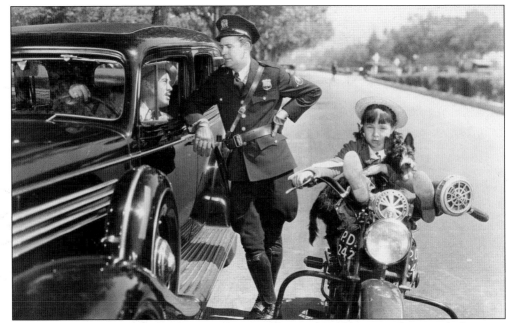

BEVERLY HILLS, 1935. Jane Withers (on motorcycle) stars as *Paddy O'Day* (Twentieth Century-Fox) on the streets of Beverly Hills. This scene was shot on Sunset Boulevard and Beverly Drive, which doubled as New York in the film. Hal K. Dawson is the motorist at left, and Russ Clark is the New York Police Department motor officer.

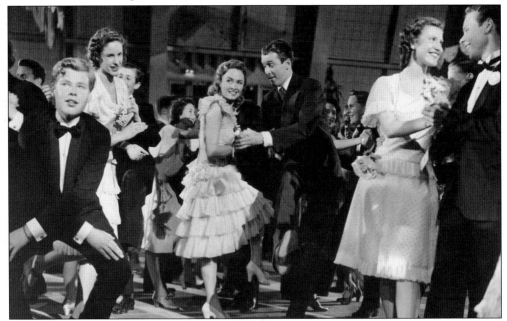

BEVERLY HILLS HIGH SCHOOL, 1946. Jimmy Stewart and Donna Reed dance on the gym floor, which opens up over a pool in the classic *It's a Wonderful Life* (RKO). Beverly Hills High School (241 Moreno Drive) had just built their new indoor pool with the moveable gymnasium floor. Director Frank Capra utilized this feature as part of the scene where many on the dance floor fall or jump into the pool when it opens unexpectedly.

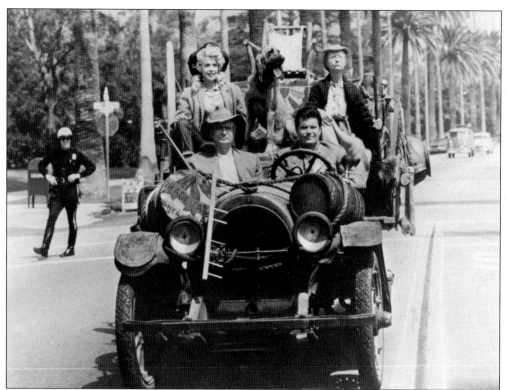

BEVERLY HILLS, 1962. The Beverly Hillbillies (Buddy Ebsen, Irene Ryan, Donna Douglas, and Max Baer Jr.) load up their truck and move to Beverly . . . Hills, that is. Note the police officer holding back traffic for the filming on Beverly Drive at Elevado Avenue. It was a short drive to the hillbillies' new "Californy" mansion, as their Ozarks shanty in the show's credits sequence was actually located a few miles away in Franklin Canyon, just off of Coldwater Canyon in Beverly Hills.

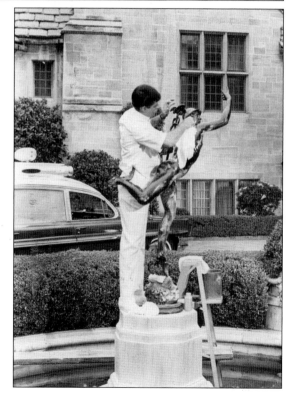

GREYSTONE PARK, 1964. Jerry Lewis polishes up a bronze fountain statue in the Greystone inner auto court in *The Disorderly Orderly* (Paramount). The mansion and the grounds were extensively used by the production and played a mental institution. The Greystone Mansion, completed in 1929, was built of Indiana limestone with a slate roof. It was purchased by the City of Beverly Hills in 1965 as a public park and water reservoir.

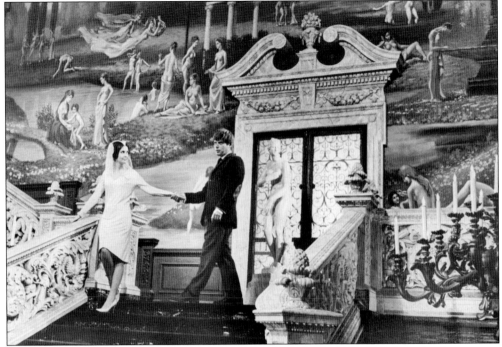

GREYSTONE MANSION, 1965. Tony Richardson's *The Loved One* used the old Doheny family mansion, Greystone, extensively as the Whispering Glades Funeral Home. Here Anjanette Comer and Robert Morse are on a tour of the property, which in reality was once the home of Edward (Ned) L. Doheny Jr. Television shows shot on the grounds include *Dark Shadows*, *Murder She Wrote*, and *Columbo*. Recent films include *X-Men*, *The Prestige*, *Spider-Man 3* and *There Will Be Blood*.

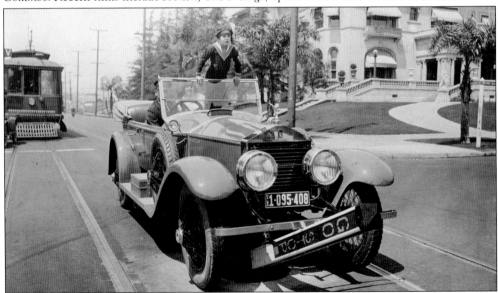

WILSHIRE BOULEVARD AND VERMONT AVENUE, 1924. Child star Jackie Coogan performs in a scene from *Little Robinson Crusoe* (Metro Goldwyn Pictures) at Wilshire Boulevard and Vermont Avenue, where his car has hit a traffic stoplight. At the top right on the northwest corner is the famous Allen Hancock estate.

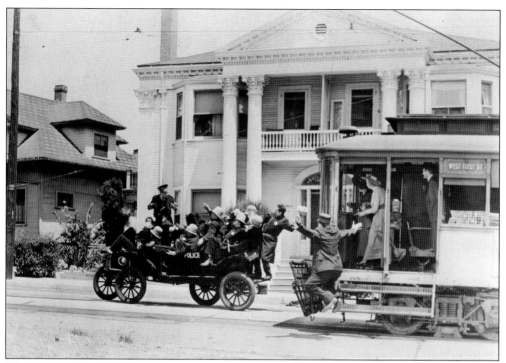

WEST FIRST STREET, 1939. Here is a re-creation of the Keystone Kops filming a scene on West First Street for *Hollywood Cavalcade* (Twentieth Century-Fox). The plot is considered by many to be based on the relationship between producer/director Mack Sennett and his comedy star Mabel Normand.

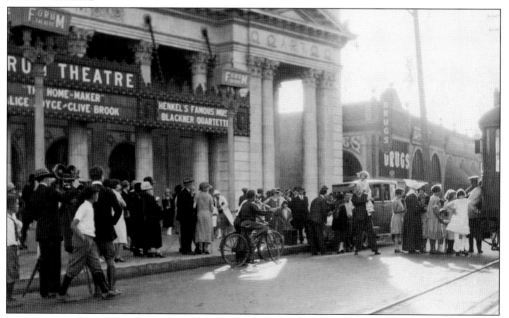

MIDCITY, 1925. A film production is being shot in front of the newly opened Forum Theatre at 4050 West Pico Boulevard east of Crenshaw Boulevard. Designed by architect Edward J. Borgmeyer in the ancient Roman style, the Forum has since been converted into a Korean church.

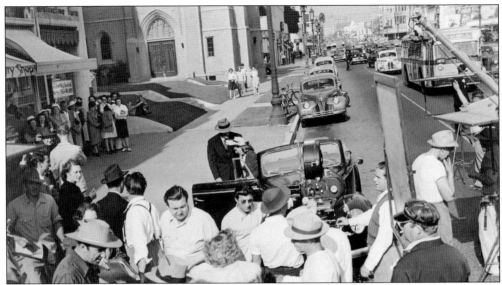

WILSHIRE BOULEVARD NEAR WESTERN AVENUE, 1942. Richard Arlen and Wendy Barrie exit a car while preparing to shoot a scene for *Submarine Alert* (Paramount). This production was promoted by studio publicists as part of a wartime campaign to "conserve set materials . . . [by] going back to using real street scenes in the movies." This location was at St. Andrews Place and Wilshire Boulevard, just two blocks west of the Wiltern Theatre.

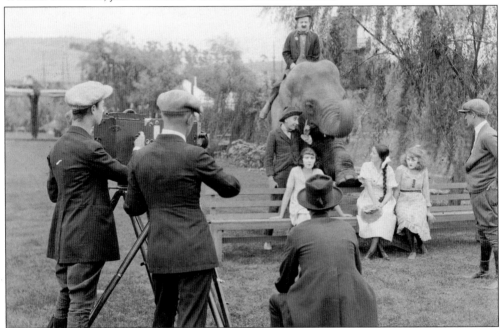

LINCOLN PARK, 1915. Al Christie directs silent comedian Larry Semon and his sidekick Eddie Dunn (on the elephant) for a Christie Comedy in Lincoln Park. Once known as Eastlake Park, this East Los Angeles recreational area featured a lake and was originally created in the late 19th century. The park became very popular with the neighborhood surrounding Mission Road in 1913 when the Selig Polyscope Company of Edendale opened an adjacent studio zoo (from where this elephant may have been rented).

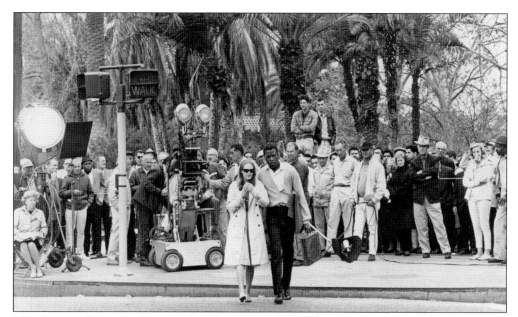

MacArthur Park, 1965. Crowds gather to watch the filming of *A Patch of Blue* (MGM), in which Sidney Poitier escorts blind girl Elizabeth Hartman across Wilshire Boulevard to a deli. This scene was shot near MacArthur Park, according to the film's English director, Guy Green, who was unaccustomed to local merchants asking for last-minute location fees. This frequently filmed neighborhood includes such locations as The Bryson (*The Grifters*) and the Elks Club/Park Plaza (*Chaplin*, *The Naked Gun*, and *Barton Fink*).

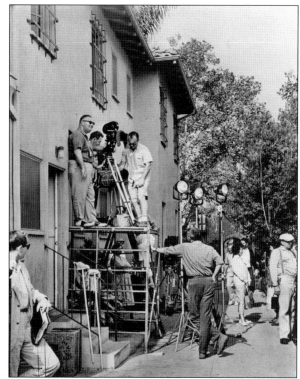

Hancock Park, 1962. Director Robert Aldrich (in sunglasses) is at work on location in the now-fashionable residential neighborhood of Hancock Park for a scene in *What Ever Happened to Baby Jane?* (Warner Bros.), starring Bette Davis and Joan Crawford. The home still stands as a private residence, and it often attracts tourists and fans of the cult classic.

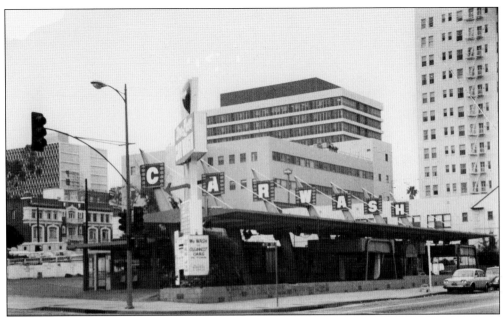

SIXTH STREET AND RAMPART BOULEVARD, 1975. Richard Pryor, George Carlin, and the Pointer Sisters starred in this film about a day in the life of employees at a *Car Wash* (Universal). The Deluxe Car Wash used for the location was torn down in the 1980s.

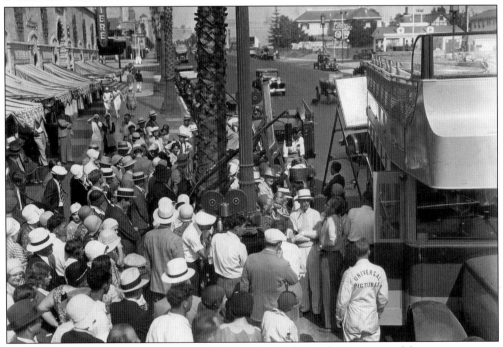

WILSHIRE BOULEVARD AND OXFORD AVENUE, 1932. On the northeast corner of this intersection, a scene is being prepared by director John Dillon for *The Cohens and Kellys in Hollywood* (Universal), starring George Sidney and Charlie Murray. The film unit is preparing to use one of Wilshire Boulevard's double-decker buses, which were very popular in the 1930s. Sidney later became a director and president of the Directors Guild of America.

Six

SAN FERNANDO VALLEY

MOVIE COUNTRY

The San Fernando Valley is a sprawling area north-northwest of Hollywood. Since much of the valley consisted of inexpensive farm and ranch land, many of the major studios and television companies located there—Universal, Disney, Warner Bros., CBS, ABC, and NBC.

Carl Laemmle was the first to realize the potential of this area. In 1912, he founded Universal Studios on a 230-acre plot of land. The area, surrounded by mountains and rugged terrain, was ideal for Westerns. By 1914, the company moved further west to Lankershim Boulevard, where Universal is still located to this day.

First National built its studio in 1918 on a Burbank lot that eventually became the world-famous Warner Bros. Studios. By 1929, Mack Sennett left Edendale and moved to the valley on a site that became Republic Pictures, and later CBS Studio Center. Ten years later, Walt Disney left his studio on Hyperion Avenue in Silver Lake and moved to Burbank.

In the late 1940s, the postwar boom drew families to the valley. Its suburban streets were able to stand in for any neighborhood in America. One example was the *Brady Bunch* house, which still stands on Dilling Street in Studio City.

Many of the studios had ranches located in the valley environs, including Paramount Ranch (*Sullivan's Travels*), Fox Ranch (*Viva Zapata!*), and Warner Bros. Ranch (*Sergeant York*).

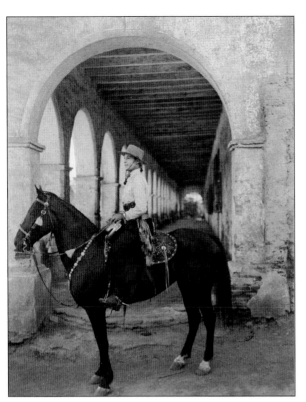

SAN FERNANDO MISSION, 1921.
Silent star Rudolph Valentino poses
in a scene for *The Four Horsemen
of the Apocalypse* (Metro) at the
San Fernando Mission, founded
in 1797. The San Fernando and
San Gabriel Missions were closest
to the studios and have been
popular locations since 1909.

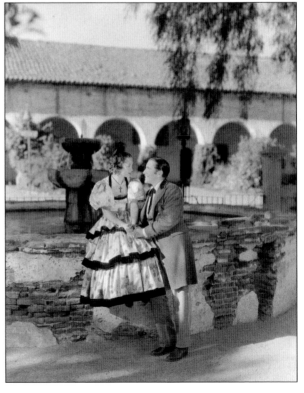

SAN FERNANDO MISSION, 1936.
John Boles and Gladys Swarthout
stand before the fountain for a
scene in the remake of *Rose of
the Rancho* (Paramount), which
takes place in California in
1952. The original *Rose of the
Rancho* was filmed in 1914 by
Cecil B. DeMille and also shot
at the same location. The studio
location departments used the
California missions as authentic
backgrounds of historic California.

SAN FERNANDO MISSION, 1939.
Luana de Alcaniz, Bill Elliott,
and Carlos Villarias (Padre)
stroll past the mission's arches
in *Frontiers of '49* (Columbia).
The mission has been used over
the years to double for Spain,
Mexico, South America, and the
early frontier days of California.

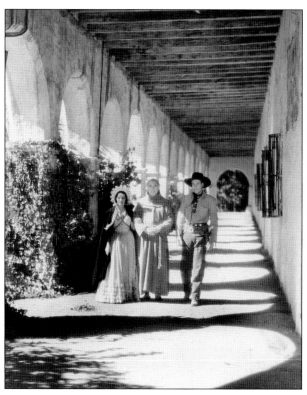

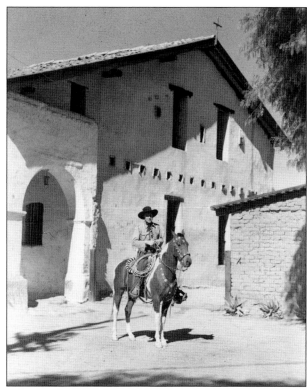

SAN FERNANDO MISSION, 1939.
Bill Elliott sits astride his horse
Dice at the east entrance to the
San Fernando Mission for a scene
in *Frontiers of '49* (Columbia).
The San Fernando Mission was
in a state of complete dilapidation
but was restored in the 1920s.

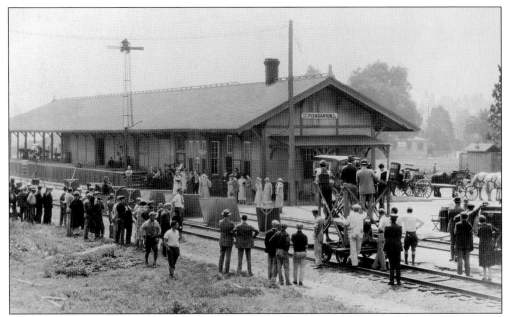

LANKERSHIM TRAIN DEPOT, 1927. North Hollywood's oldest structure, this 1895 depot at Lankershim and Chandler Boulevards posed as a rural Pleasanton train station for the Cecil B. DeMille–produced *The Country Doctor* (Pathé). The film starred Rudolph Schildkraut and Junior Coghlan and was directed by Rupert Julien.

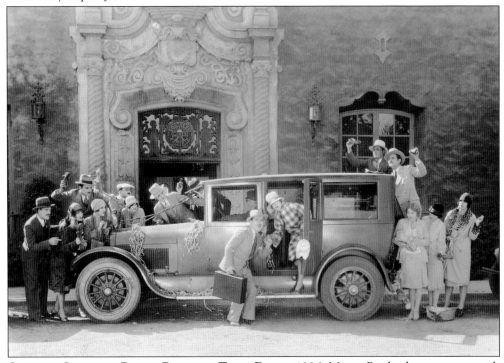

GLENDALE SOUTHERN PACIFIC RAILROAD TRAIN DEPOT, 1926. Monty Banks shoots a scene with Jean Arthur (in car) for the comedy *Horse Shoes* (Pathé). The still-standing train station was built in 1923 by the Southern Pacific Railroad and designed in the Mission Revival style.

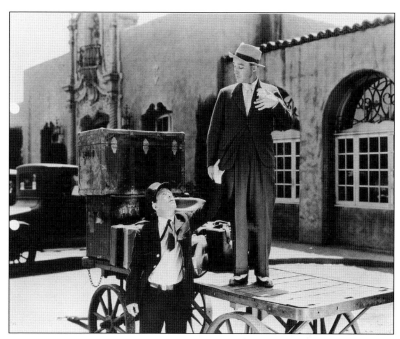

GLENDALE DEPOT, 1931. Bing Crosby plays a traveling washing machine salesman with aspirations to be a crooner in *One More Chance* (Sennett). The Glendale Southern Pacific Railroad Train Depot was a popular location close to the San Fernando Valley studios.

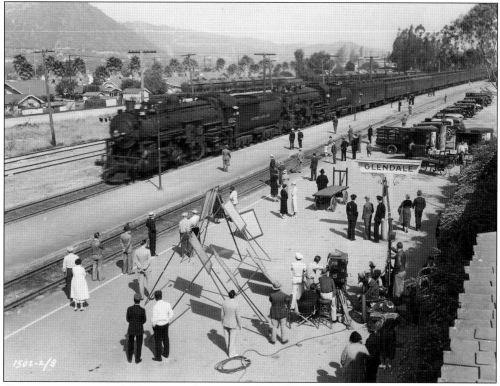

GLENDALE DEPOT, 1934. The cast and crew prepare to film a scene for the 1934 romantic comedy *Here Comes the Groom* (Paramount), starring Jack Haley and Mary Boland. The station is most famously featured in *Double Indemnity*, where Fred MacMurray helps Barbara Stanwyck dump her husband's murdered body on the train tracks.

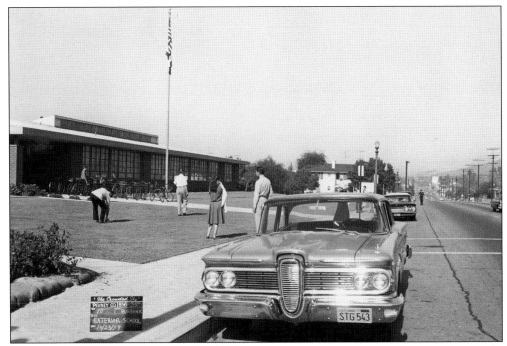

BURBANK, 1960. Pictured is an exterior shot of McCambridge Park Recreation Center for *The Crowded Sky* (Warner Bros.), a Dana Andrews-Rhonda Fleming drama. The recreation center's stage hosted Michael J. Fox's "Battle of the Bands" sequence in *Back to the Future*.

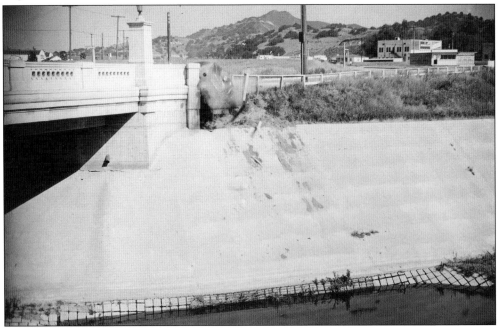

STUDIO CITY, 1936. A car crashes into the Laurel Canyon Bridge over the Los Angeles River for a scene in the film *And Sudden Death* (Paramount), starring Randolph Scott. This scene was shot at Laurel Canyon Boulevard and Valley Heart Drive in the proximity of the Republic Studios, site of today's CBS Studio Center at Ventura Boulevard and Radford Drive.

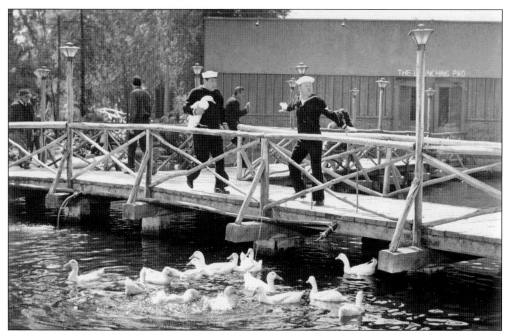

STUDIO CITY, 1961. Buddy Hackett and Mickey Rooney take Scuttlebutt the Talking Duck for a drink at Sportsmen's Lodge in *Everything's Ducky* (Columbia). The legendary hangout claimed that Clark Gable and John Wayne used to fish for their sportsmen's dinners at its trout ponds near the northeast corner of Coldwater Canyon and Ventura Boulevards.

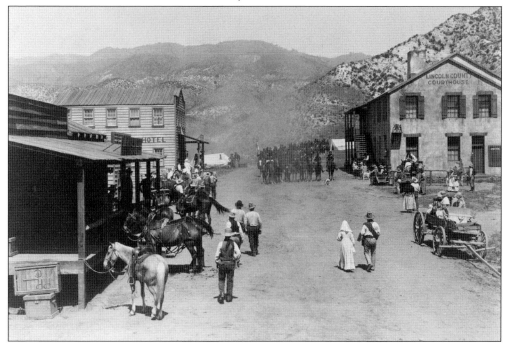

PORTER RANCH, 1930. This valley suburb once hosted a Western town set for Lincoln, New Mexico, in King Vidor's *Billy the Kid* (MGM). The film starred Wallace Beery as Pat Garrett and Johnny Mack Brown in the title role.

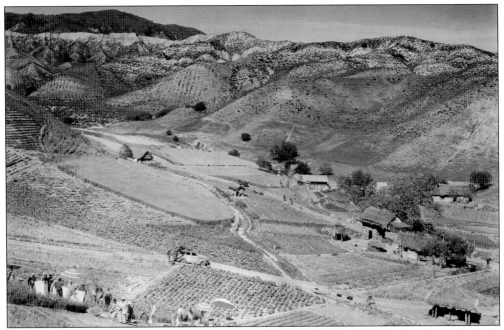

PORTER RANCH, 1937. The location of the huge farm and village site for *The Good Earth* (MGM), starring Paul Muni, was bounded by the Santa Susana Mountains. A tract of 500 acres, north of today's 118 freeway, was transformed into a Chinese farm. The neighborhood's Porter Ridge Park served as a location in the climactic chase in Steven Spielberg's *E.T.*

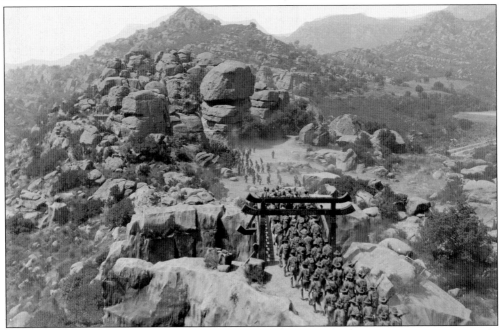

CHATSWORTH, 1926. Iverson Ranch is seen as it appeared in the 1927 release of *Tell It to the Marines* (MGM), starring Lon Chaney. The famous "Garden of the Gods" rocks of the Iverson Ranch doubled as China. The rocks are still recognizable today, but most of the ranch is hidden amidst development.

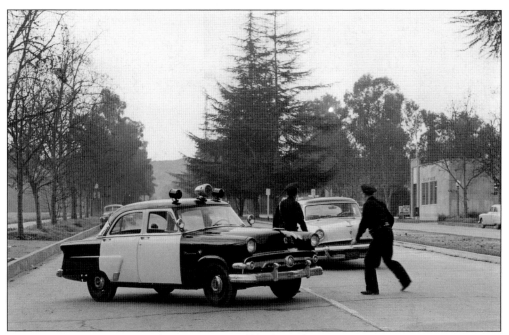

WOODLAND HILLS, 1956. Police set up a roadblock in the effort to catch robbers on location on Topanga Canyon Boulevard and Del Valle Street (south of Ventura Boulevard) for the crime drama *Man is Armed* (Republic), starring Dane Clark.

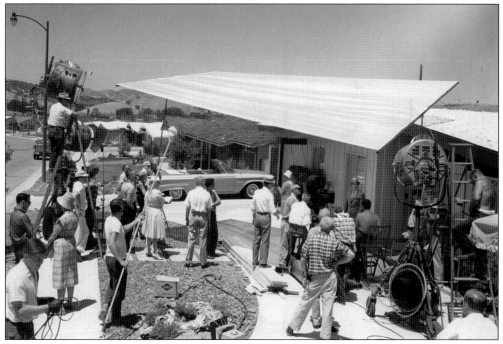

WOODLAND HILLS, 1961. Bob Hope plays a *Bachelor in Paradise* (MGM) who romances suburban housewives Lana Turner and Paula Prentiss. The movie's ranch homes, newly built when the film was made, can still be found near the intersection of Valmar Road and Mulholland Drive in Woodland Hills.

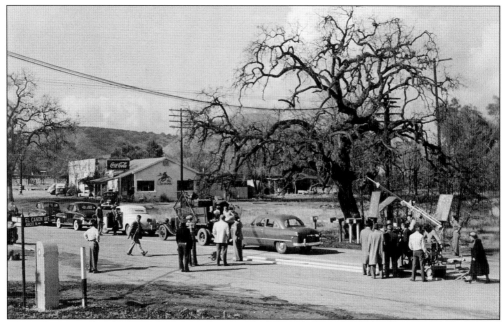

OLD TOWN CALABASAS, 1949. This rural area at the corner of Calabasas Road and El Canon Avenue, across the street from the Leonis Adobe and the Sagebrush Cantina, appears in the film noir *Take One False Step* (Universal), starring William Powell and Shelley Winters. Today the Motion Picture and Television Fund facilities stand near the site.

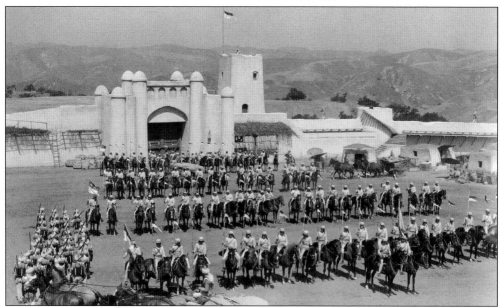

UPPER LAS VIRGENES CANYON, 1936. Ahmanson Ranch's Lasky Mesa, just north of Calabasas off of Las Virgenes Road, provided an expansive setting for *The Charge of the Light Brigade* (Warner Bros.). The property was sold to the Santa Monica Mountains Conservancy and other agencies in 2003. Hiking trails now traverse this pristine open space, which is still used for filming large-scale set pieces (the bridge ambush in *Mission: Impossible III* and the flaming weed farmhouse in *Pineapple Express*).

Seven

OTHER UNIQUE LOCATIONS

CLASSIC HOLLYWOOD LANDSCAPES

Several distinct sites in Los Angeles County have proven to be memorable locations for filming over the last 100 years. Many of these extraordinary hideaways are off the beaten path, providing filmmakers with privacy in a host of scenic areas.

Santa Catalina Island is only about 20 miles from the mainland, but it seems like a world away. As the city of Los Angeles began to rapidly develop, Catalina remained pristine and devoid of modern intrusions, such as telephone wires, streetcars, or traffic. It provided an isolated and beautiful setting that could easily substitute for Hong Kong, Greece, the South Seas, or the French Riviera. Between 1915 and 1935, more than 150 films were shot on the island, including *The Black Pirate, Old Ironsides, Island of Lost Souls, Rain, Treasure Island,* and *Mutiny on the Bounty.*

Franklin Canyon highlights include pine trees and a lake tucked away in the mountains between Beverly Hills and the San Fernando Valley. The area has been used in films such as *It Happened One Night* and *The Manchurian Candidate.*

A article published in *Cinema Review* dated 1924 claimed that any kind of unique location could be found in Southern California, including "rugged mountains and pastoral valleys, country lanes and city streets, jungles and deserts, every imaginable kind of a building from castles and mansions to hovels and dog houses. All as near as possible to the studio." Even after decades of development in L.A., this industry observation is still accurate.

Here's to the next 100 years of location filming in Los Angeles County!

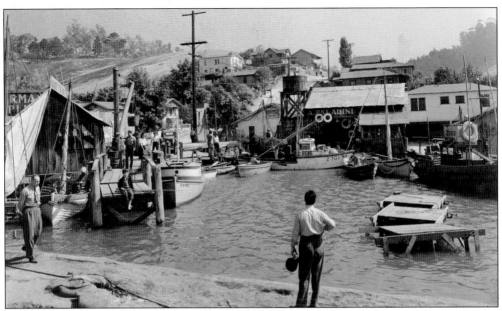

Chavez Ravine—Los Angeles, 1945. An area of Chavez Ravine adjacent to Elysian Park is transformed into a fishing village for *A Medal for Benny* (Paramount), cowritten by John Steinbeck. Chavez Ravine was a large Latino community but in the late 1940s became the center of a raging political debate. A portion of the land was cleared and residents evicted before it was developed into Dodger Stadium.

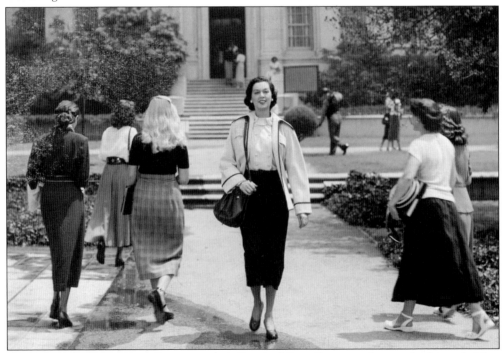

Eagle Rock—Occidental College, 1949. Rosalind Russell stars as the uptight dean of a New England university in *A Woman of Distinction* (Columbia), filmed at Occidental College. Since the 1920s, it has been a popular location for movies like *Clueless*, *Pat and Mike*, and *Horse Feathers*.

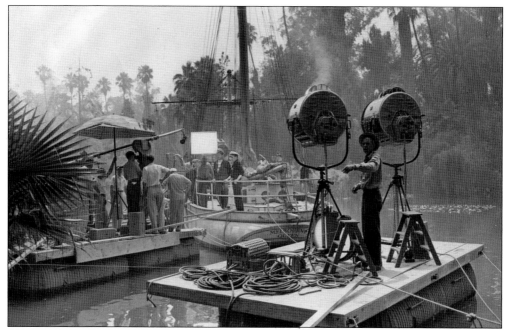

LOS ANGELES COUNTY ARBORETUM—ARCADIA, 1948. The arboretum's lagoon is the center of action with John Wayne in *Wake of the Red Witch*. The arboretum's 1880s Queen Anne cottage has played a remote hideaway in *Objective Burma*, television's *Fantasy Island*, and *Meet the Fockers*. It is located at 301 North Baldwin Avenue in Arcadia, California.

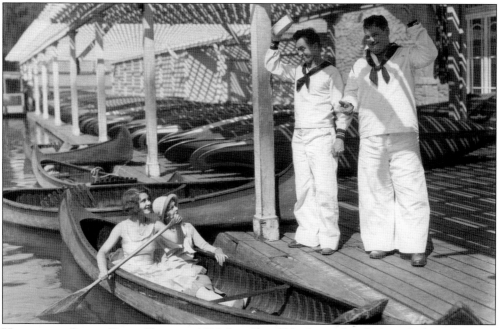

HOLLENBECK PARK—BOYLE HEIGHTS, 1929. Laurel and Hardy stand at the boat docks and prepare to join their flapper dates for a canoe ride that is destined for chaos in *Men 'O War* (MGM). Hollenbeck Park was used as a park location since the early 1910s and is located on Boyle Avenue and St. Louis Street, east of downtown L.A.

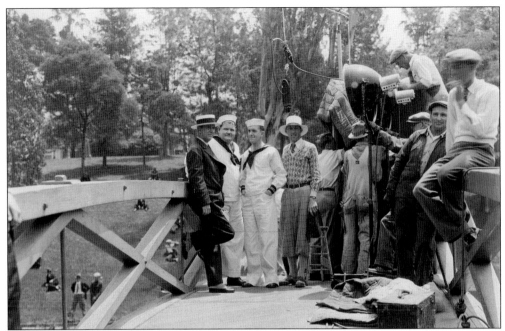

HOLLENBECK PARK BRIDGE—BOYLE HEIGHTS, 1929. Laurel and Hardy, with director Lewis R. Foster and the crew, prepare to film a scene for the film *Men 'O War* (MGM) on the Hollenbeck Park Bridge. Note the addition of a microphone for this early sound film shot on location.

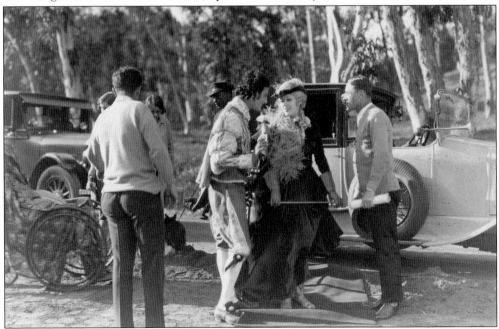

ELYSIAN PARK—LOS ANGELES, 1928. Marion Davies arrives on location at Elysian Park to shoot a scene for the comedy *Show People* (MGM). This lighthearted film about life in the motion picture business featured several authentic locales, including Hollywood Boulevard and the MGM studio lot, as well as cameos by Charlie Chaplin, John Gilbert, Douglas Fairbanks, and William S. Hart.

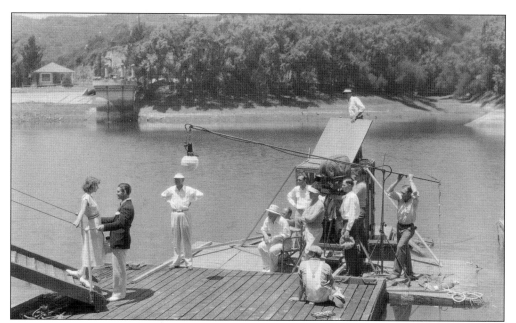

FRANKLIN CANYON, 1931. Greta Garbo, Clark Gable, director Robert Z. Leonard, and crew film a scene for *Susan Lenox: Her Fall and Rise* (MGM) at Franklin Canyon Reservoir. This was the only pairing of Garbo and Gable. Located next to Coldwater Canyon, Franklin Canyon is located at 2600 Franklin Canyon Drive in Beverly Hills.

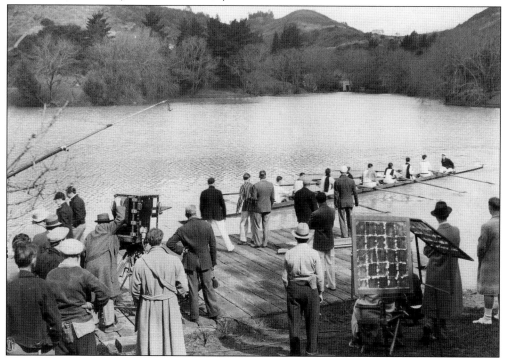

FRANKLIN CANYON, 1938. Franklin Canyon Reservoir stands in for England in *Four Men and a Prayer* (Twentieth Century-Fox), starring David Niven. John Ford directs this scene featuring an Oxford rowing team that was actually manned by a UCLA crew.

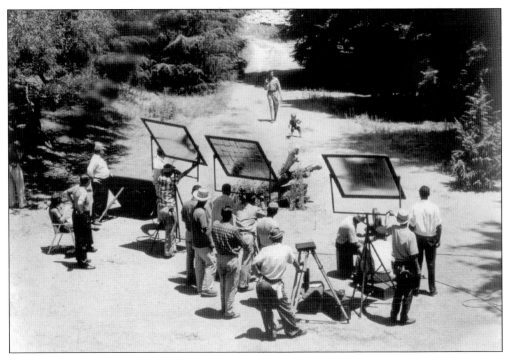

FRANKLIN CANYON, 1960. Andy Griffith strolls the Franklin Canyon woods to shoot the famous whistling opening to television's *The Andy Griffith Show*. He appeared each week with his television son, played by Ronny Howard, the future Oscar-winning director. The famous scene was shot at the north end of Franklin Canyon Reservoir.

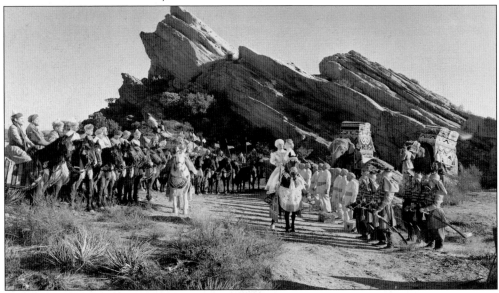

VASQUEZ ROCKS, 1945. One of the most popular film locations in Southern California, Vasquez Rocks has been used as many exotic backgrounds, from alien planets to the Middle East, as seen here in *A Thousand And One Nights* (Columbia). The rock formations feel remote, even though they are located within Los Angeles's 30-mile zone, just off the Antelope Valley Freeway near the Santa Clarita Valley town of Agua Dulce.

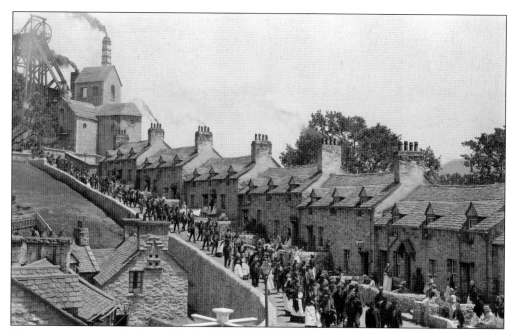

MALIBU CREEK STATE PARK, 1940. This Calabasas-adjacent property provides the setting for a Welsh mining village in John Ford's Oscar-winning best picture *How Green Was My Valley*. The set no longer survives, but the hill can be viewed from the park's second parking lot.

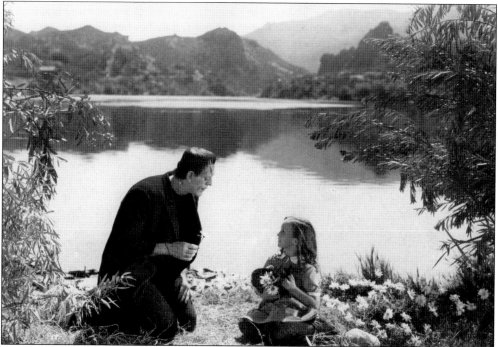

MALIBOU LAKE—AGOURA, 1931. Boris Karloff and child actress Marilyn Harris throw daisies into the water at Malibou Lake for a scene in *Frankenstein* (Universal). This exclusive hideaway, west of Malibu Creek State Park, also appears in Charlie Chaplin's *The Great Dictator*, *The Bad Seed*, and *Must Love Dogs*.

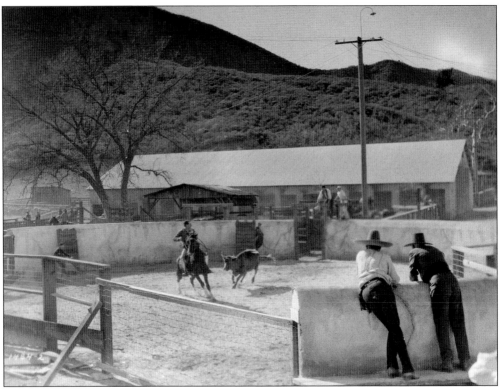

Paramount Ranch—Agoura, 1930. *The Trumpet Blows*, starring George Raft, was set in old Mexico but shot at the Paramount Ranch. Sugarloaf Peak can be seen in the background. The barn was built in 1927 when Paramount first acquired the ranch, and it remains standing today. It was remodeled as a soundstage during the filming of the television series *Dr. Quinn, Medicine Woman.*

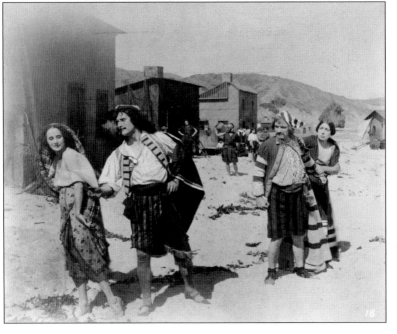

Catalina Island, 1916. Famed ballerina Anna Pavlova stars in *The Dumb Girl of Portici* (Universal), her only acting appearance. Early filmmakers discovered that Catalina Island offered stunning geography within a close, convenient distance to the studios in nearby Los Angeles.

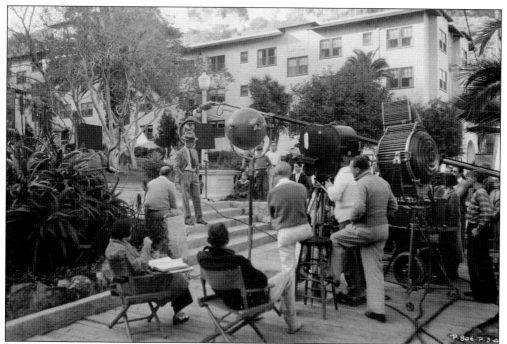

CATALINA ISLAND—DESCANSO BEACH, 1935. Actor James Gleason and crew film in front of Descanso Beach's luxurious Hollywood hangout, Hotel St. Catherine, for the Robert Benchley–scripted suspense-comedy *Murder on a Honeymoon* (RKO). The hotel was torn down in 1966. Today Descanso Bay features a beach club open to the public, where people can enjoy a drink, lounge in the sand, and admire the dramatic views.

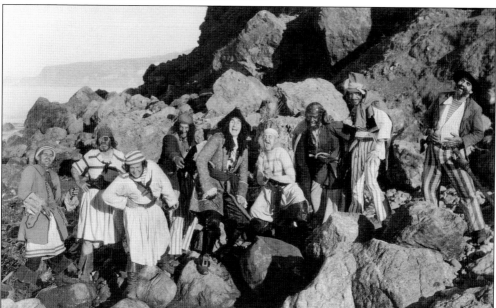

CATALINA ISLAND, 1925. Ernest Torrence (Captain Hook) and Edward Kipling (Smee) pose with their pirate crew on the coast rocks in the silent film version of *Peter Pan* (Paramount), starring Betty Bronson in the title role.

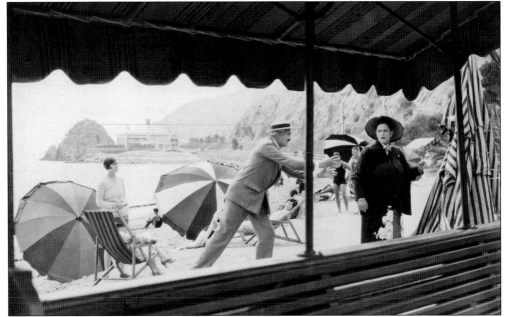

CATALINA ISLAND, 1927. Glenn Tyron and Patsy Ruth Miller star in A *Hero for a Night* (Universal), filmed on Catalina Island. Sugarloaf Rock and the old Sugarloaf Casino can be seen in the distance.

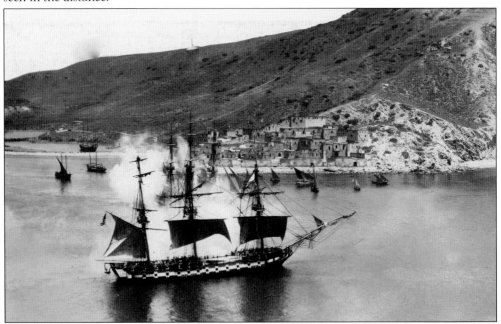

CATALINA HARBOR, 1926. So many movies were shot in the Isthmus/Two Harbors area of Catalina that it was nicknamed "The Isthmus Movie Colony" by the 1930s. Catalina Island doubled for the North African coast in *Old Ironsides,* where an American warship battles Barbary Pirates in the 18th century. The film starred Charles Farrell and Esther Ralston and used the Chinese junk *Ning-Po* (today one can see parts of the wreck at Ballast Point at extreme low tide) and other actual ships in and around the island.

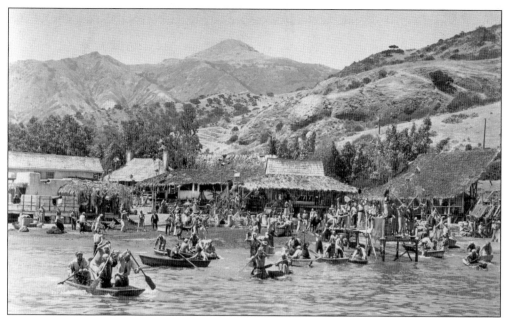

CATALINA ISLAND, 1938. Cecil B. DeMille recreated the War of 1812 on Catalina Island for *The Buccaneer* (Paramount), starring Fredric March. Here is the re-creation of the Barataria settlement at White's Landing on the island. Other locations on the island were used for the Battle of New Orleans.

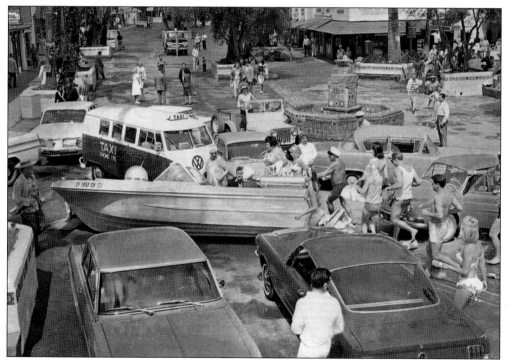

CATALINA ISLAND, 1966. Rod Taylor (center, seated in the boat) dry-docks on Avalon's Crescent Avenue in the Doris Day comedy *The Glass Bottom Boat* (MGM). The production company took over the entire tourist area in Avalon to create this comedic traffic jam.

DISCOVER THOUSANDS OF LOCAL HISTORY BOOKS FEATURING MILLIONS OF VINTAGE IMAGES

Arcadia Publishing, the leading local history publisher in the United States, is committed to making history accessible and meaningful through publishing books that celebrate and preserve the heritage of America's people and places.

Find more books like this at
www.arcadiapublishing.com

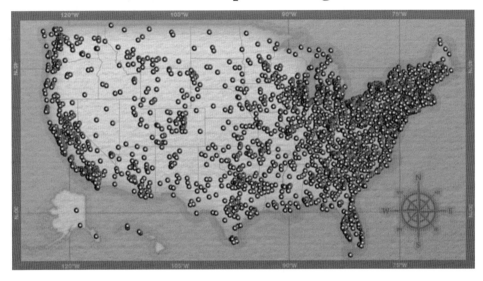

Search for your hometown history, your old stomping grounds, and even your favorite sports team.

Consistent with our mission to preserve history on a local level, this book was printed in South Carolina on American-made paper and manufactured entirely in the United States. Products carrying the accredited Forest Stewardship Council (FSC) label are printed on 100 percent FSC-certified paper.

MADE IN THE
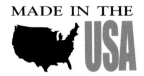
USA